AFTER THE ALTER: LIVING THE BIBLE OUT LOUD

MARY L. HEMMINGWAY

Copyright © 2018 Mary L. Hemmingway

All rights reserved.

Published by Claire Aldin Publications, LLC
P. O. Box 453, Southfield, MI 48037

Book design by: Sow Graphics & Publications, LLC

Edited by Shairon L. Taylor, SLT Inspirations, LLC

Unless otherwise indicated, all scriptures are taken from the Holy Bible, King James Version, which is in the public domain.

No portion of this book may be reproduced, stored in a retrieval system, or transmitted in any form or by any means – electronic, mechanical, photocopy, recording, or any other – except for brief quotations in printed reviews, without the prior written permission of the author.

Library of Congress Control Number: 2018951872

ISBN-13: 978-0-9996840-6-1

Printed in the United States Of America

FOREWORD

For many, the church is a place of healing, a place of refuge. It's the comfort in the midst of a storm or peace in times of turmoil. It's the filling station – the place where the empty, the broken, and the destitute go to be refueled. Week after week, parishioners worldwide gather at their respective places of worship to hear from God. They go to get recharged. They go to get another hit, another fix. Because something, somewhere down on the inside, tells them that if they can just get to the church, everything will be alright. And it will, but not automatically.

So many times, churches focus on the salvation message, but omit the deliverance message. It is absolutely vital to talk about the cross. It's key that people know about the death, burial, and resurrection of the Lord, Jesus Christ. It is equally critical that the church lead people to a relationship – not religion – with Christ Jesus. But once a person has committed their life to Christ, then what? The Bible says in 2 Corinthians 5:17 *"Therefore if any man be in Christ, he is a new creature: old things are passed away; behold, all things are become new.* So essentially, when a person dedicates their life to Christ, they are born again. It's like they are a newborn in the spirit. They don't know this new world. They don't necessarily know how to function in it. Just like a newborn baby has to learn how to crawl, then walk, then run, when a person commits their life to Christ for the first time, they need help.

While they may know "church rhetoric" or religious practices, Christ ultimately wants a personal relationship with each and every individual Christian. Just like a marriage or a long-time friendship, relationship takes time and it takes consistent communication. This is what makes *After the Alter: Living the Bible Out Loud* different from every Christian book on the market. It speaks to the after effects of salvation. Once you get past the "honeymoon phase" of saying, "Yes!" to God, you have to live. Trials are going to come. Trouble will appear at your doorstep. Being a follower of Christ and being saved does not exempt you from struggles, strongholds and life's issues. It simply makes those times much more significant when you realize "*...that all things work together for good to* *them that love God, to them who are the called according to His purpose"* (Romans 8:28).

This life-changing book is critical to the kingdom of God. While many people are saved, and they attend church every Sunday, they don't have power. They don't have the power to fight or war against the enemy. They don't have the tools to properly complete their God-given assignments and many of them still live in fear. But when one surrenders to God at an altar, the great 'alter' takes place! In that moment, a person's eternal life is secure. It's locked and confirmed; however, they still live in a natural world until their assignment is complete in the earth. While many people dance around the elephants in the room and skeletons in the closet, this book deals with life's issues and past head on. Prepare to unpack your spiritual baggage. Open your mind. Open your eyes and ears. We're going on a journey and ready to take flight, but I promise, you'll and safely. Congratulations! You've just stepped into the next level in God.

You've been to the altar, now prepare to be altered!

~Tenita "Bestseller" Johnson

TO THE READERS

Greetings! I am so glad you chose to read this wonderful book that my Father and I wrote for you. It is purposely written without the grandeur of eloquent words. It's an easy read…conversational, as if we're conversing over morning coffee. I pray you will peruse it often as a companion with your Bible. I want you to apprehend it, comprehend it, and then share it. This book is written for all people, all races, to *every* man. We can no longer hold pastors and preachers hostage in our minds for the responsibility of us learning and living for God. The Bible admonishes us to read, study, and talk to God for ourselves. Therefore, the Father tapped me on my shoulder to write; that He, through me, can assist you with the basics of living life in sanctification.

This book is written for the fence swinger, new convert, seasoned saint and the weary. I've compiled just a few snapshots of principles for living separated from your old self. I'm teaching on the trials of life in salvation that others say are barely preached over the pulpit anymore. It's time to be real about it. Let's be clear; the devil is *real*, and he's after our physical and spiritual life. The devil has the pulpit of the radio, television, Facebook, Twitter, and all other facets of media. If the devil can use these to draw the souls from Christ; we (the preachers of God) must use these same methods to draw the souls back to God.

I believe most will appreciate a strong and honest look at the peaks and valleys traveled in this life. You will find that you're not the only one struggling. However, if I wrote to every circumstance, situation and battle, I imagine there would be no ending to the books that could be written. After all, many are still being written, and by the time you mature in Him; you will have a few nuggets to contribute yourself.

~Mary L. Hemmingway

CONTENTS

	Introduction	9
1	My Soul Can't Wait	11
2	Insurance Policy	20
3	A Faithless Generation	40
4	People of War	57
5	Church Flow	85
6	Forgiving Past the Pain	97
7	Changing Altars	113
8	Mind Games	122
9	Godhead	138
10	What's In A Name?	145
11	The Blood	150
12	Baggage Claim	154
13	Switch Blade	173
14	Hole In My Pocket	191
15	Body Parts	216

INTRODUCTION

It's Sunday morning and the preacher is coming to the close of his sermon. As he vigorously pounds his fist on the podium, the congregation screams, "Preach, pastor!" as the music plays thunderously in the background. Your heart begins to beat harder than an African drum just before war. Your fists are clammy and your knees are shaking, too. At that moment you ask yourself, "What's going on with me? I've come to this church plenty of times and I have never felt this way before!"

"Will there be one?" the pastor calls. It almost rings muffled in your ears. You can see the preacher's mouth moving, but you can't hear him. The voice of God seemly is the only voice you hear. In what seems like a trance, afterwards, you're in the upper room being submerged in the baptismal pool. You and the Father are now spiritually married, consummated through your acceptance and belief of the Gospel and on the death, burial, and resurrection of Jesus Christ.

Now, days and months have gone by and you're yet dealing with struggles in your flesh.

You are not alone. Come and go with me to a short catechism class entitled *After the Alter: Living the Bible Out Loud*. It is sure to meet you in the place where you battle. After this, no more sitting in service with that gnawing thought running through your mind.

Pastor, Sunday after Sunday you teach on many things, including the gift of tongues. But pastor, how do I live when the tongues are *done?*

1

MY SOUL CAN'T WAIT

In the medical profession, no matter what field you're in whether it is psychology, psychiatry, mental health or substance abuse counseling, the first step to the process of getting help is to admit that you have a problem. Most are aware that this is a rule in all areas of human services, including Narcotics, Alcoholics, Gamblers, and Sex Addiction Anonymous. In the process of admittance, it helps one to verbalize it and come face to face with themselves and their hidden addiction. Professionals will tell you that in order to sincerely beat the addiction there are three things you must disassociate yourself from: people, places and things. This means the people you associate with must change because of your addiction. The places you go must change because of your addiction. Finally, the things you used to do when you would go to those places and see those people must cease because of your addiction. If not, your reckless past will soon repeat itself. Because you have an addiction, your mind is addicted, obsessed. People, places and things are the three battles in your mind you must be determined to conquer.

Programs like these and others have been based on the acceptance of a 12-step program to get healthy. Relatives, friends, parents, children and even your bosses have noticed a change. Most people believe they are still "normal" simply because they can't see themselves outside of themselves. Usually, we as people have a false sense of who we really have become. Unfortunately, because we are living in it, we never notice that it has consumed our very existence. Beloved, when you finally glance at yourself in the mirror, with an honest eye, you'll admit to yourself: *I am an addict*. No matter what the addiction may be, you have one gripping you like a pair of vice grips on the end of the screw that changes the channel on the small television sitting on top of the larger broken television.

Your life is a mess! You're spiraling out of control and must seek help before it's too late. You're bound up without hope, so it seems. Some might even say that it's too late for you because you've been out there too long to come back now. But, there is an answer: *Jesus*! All He needs is your confession. Many are familiar with the order of court. In a court system, before a confession or statement is made, the bailiff asks the person on the stand to put their hand on the Holy Bible; then the bailiff asks, "Do you promise to tell the truth, the whole truth and nothing but the truth, so help you God?" Of course, the answer is always yes; but most people start lying even before the cross examination has begun. Will he or she give up and just confess? Probably not! Sometimes, it's totally up to the character and integrity of a person. One can never tell sometimes until the very end. Confession, confession, confession; it is good for the soul. Some say it's good because confession eases the mind. In the body of Christ, we know that it's written in 1 John 1:9 that *"if we confess our sins, he is faithful and just to forgive us our sins and cleanse us from all unrighteousness"*. The key word here is cleanse, which is good for the soul. To cleanse is to purge, to change us from dirty to clean; this directs us towards the rebirth.

Let us dwell there for a moment. The above

scripture states, cleanse us from all unrighteousness, but it does not say save us. There is more to being saved or getting saved than just confessing your sins. That's just the beginning. Sin brings a numbness and arrogance when you've been a great participator; after all, we were *shapen in iniquity and conceived in sin* (Psalm 51:5). This makes it difficult for confession to take place because your mind can become seared (numb) to sin. You call wrong, right and right, wrong; it's a vicious cycle. When one has played the sin game so long, it becomes the norm. We will continue to explore that thought as we walk into the next chapter. Let's keep it moving on the road to confessions.

The part of the passage in James 5:16 which says, *confess your faults one to another, and pray one for another, that ye may be healed,"* has reigned supreme in the Catholic religion. The parishioners confess to a man (priest) in a box (no disrespect intended) to relieve themselves of the burdens they carried alone. However, we have a Father, who will carry those burdens for us in Jesus Christ. *"Come unto me, all ye that labour and are heavy laden, and I will give you rest.*

Take my yoke upon you, and learn of me; for I am meek and lowly in heart: and ye shall find rest unto your souls" (Matthew 11:28-29). This wonderful ability came when Jesus died. His death ripped the divider between us and the Father, thereby, we can go to the Father Himself without the partition. God, through Jesus, destroyed or tore the veil and the Bible declares that now we can come to the throne of grace boldly and petition the Father without the help of a priest. Rest from the burdens we have carried wrought from sins, they are no more. Nobody can give us peace like the Father can... grateful. So, as you are reading this, have you given your soul rest and confessed yet?

The Bible tells us to "*...lay aside every weight, and the sin which doth so easily beset us, and let us run with patience the race that is set before us, looking to Jesus the author and finisher of our faith...*", (Hebrews 12:1-2a). Have you struck up a conversation between you and the Father today? Gentle one, I am not just talking to the unsaved, but the saved also. We can't get caught up in the "once saved, always saved" aspect; that is a flat-out lie. Yes, I said it! The truth is the truth. Here's some Bible on it. If once saved always saved were true, why would the Father say in Jeremiah 3:14 that He is married to the backslider? It is because He knew we were going to slide back faster than a car rolling backwards in neutral without any brakes; reverting back is in us to do. We do things, shame God and then say, "Well, God knows my heart." Yes, you are exactly right, He does! He knows our hearts are extremely wicked without His grace. We, (the church) backslide all the time and forget that "we" need to confess and return to God daily. Again, *this book* was not just written for the unsaved, but the saved alike.

Where the Word speaks of laying aside every weight, it implies that the lifestyle of sin carries a weight with it. It's heavy, you know. The more sin we invite into our lives, the heavier the weight becomes. Let me say it like this: you are a person who is overweight and have a condition with your knees. Against the advice of your doctors, you continue to eat unhealthy and exercise is far from you. Of course, as you continue to do this, your metabolism continues to slow down, your knees become weaker and can no longer handle the weight. A plummet is coming! In other words, be assured that if the issue is not resolved, your knees will buckle under the weight of it all. Sin has a weight to it! Therefore, lay it aside, put it down, throw it away, and stop it! Sin creates that weight that easily distracts you from confessing and living a sinless lifestyle in God, in an imperfect world. We should all be after the heart and attention of God.

Now to get God's attention, you might want to start where David did. Psalm 51:1 says, *"have mercy upon me, O God, according to your loving-kindness: according to the multitude of thy tender mercies blot out my transgressions"*. Read it at your leisure. Now you have a conversation going between the two of you. You want His eyes to turn towards you. Get His attention by confessing your heart unto Him. In Jeremiah 29, God says that when we seek Him, we shall find Him if we seek Him with our whole heart.

For example, in business deals, the proprietors or dealers are not listening to a buyer until they say something worth listening to-that one word, phrase or amount they want to hear. Once that is spoken, the buyer has their attention. In their mind or even out loud, the owner may say, "Go on, I'm listening." Something the buyer said struck a chord with them. In your confession, when you speak to the Father from His Word, His ears tune into your voice, the words you have spoken. You've gotten His attention. If you're thinking right now, what exactly did King David say in the book? Well, we will cover that in the next passage.

Back to King David…there's more! David was one of the greatest, richest and most powerful Kings in Israel; however, David confessed to God after He sent Nathan the prophet to speak David after he had sinned with Bathsheba. Isn't it interesting that her name was *Bath-sheba*? Bathsheba was taking a bath on the rooftop of the house and because David had a lust spirit and womanizing spirit, that's where all the trouble started. Well… not exactly. David was not where he was supposed to be. He should have been fighting in a war. But that's a book for another time. After David was uncovered in his sin, Psalm 51 was birthed. Psalm 51:3 says, *"For I acknowledge my transgressions:* (I confess-recognize) *and my sin is ever before me* (I keep it in the forefront of my mind that I do not do this type of sin before you again)". David had no problem confessing unto the Father. David had a great calling upon his life. He was what we would consider a "good boy." The Bible says that God considered David as a "man after His own heart." Why? Because David had no issues with worshipping, talking or confessing his wrongs to God, and that pulled on God's heartstrings. Confession here was good for the soul.

Did you know God has a confession of His own? Here it is in Jeremiah 31:3 *"Yea, I have loved thee with an everlasting love: therefore with lovingkindness have I drawn thee"*. He also confessed His love for us, by sending and giving His only beloved Son to die and save us from our sins. Since Jesus is the Savior of the world, why should we be bound? You and I don't have to be, if we remember to continue to confess our wrongs as we live this walk of salvation; *After the Alter*. This is a good place to confess your faults. Jesus will wait and then whisper in a soft kind voice, *After the Alter* experience.... *Amen.*

2

INSURANCE POLICY

Many years ago I remember a television commercial aired in black and white. This commercial spoke of getting your Last Will and Testament in order. This commercial showed a family who wasn't prepared for the sudden death of their loved one. Although I was too young at the time to understand it, I would hear my mother constantly saying, "I don't want to ever be the one" or "I don't ever want my children passing a hat around begging and borrowing money for my funeral." She detested that!

As times changed, African Americans matriculated into Hollywood and were receiving just as many callbacks for commercials as Caucasians. African Americans began to be in demand; we were seeing them in all types of commercials. Well, the commercial I mentioned earlier signed an African American man-tall, handsome, not only to be the sultry voice, but also to be the face of this internationally known insurance company, Allstate. Their motto has always been, "You're in good hands with Allstate." Even if you didn't care for the insurance company, his soothing voice and strong smile grabbed your attention right away. It stands to reason, that if you gotta have it, the black face assured you that your family would be taken care of financially in the death of your loved one, with no regrets. The gentleman's voice made you comfortable with purchasing this insurance even though you've never seen the president or vice president of this company. You bought it totally on faith. But, wait; there's more!

This brings me to the story in Luke 15 where a certain man had two sons. The younger son had premeditated his own eviction in his heart and was scheduling the perfect day for the bailiff (his father) to come. The son allowed the conversations with his friends to draw him away from the love and covering of his father, long before he actually vacated the premises. The lure of *the lust of the flesh, the lust of the eye, and the pride of life* (1 John 2:16) began to build in his heart. This brought forth a desire to sin that spiraled out of control in his mind. Every night when his boys came by to kick it (21st century paraphrasing) and discuss about all the women they'd meet and all the excitement being away from parental guidance, the son began to fantasize about how wonderful it could be and what it would be like to be on his own, ravished by the night life.

Well, the Bible tells us in Luke that the son finally built up enough nerve to ask his father for *his* inheritance--the gifts and monies he and his brother would receive after the death of their father. Do you mind if I use my imagination here for a moment? I can imagine the father being appalled, offended and even hurt at his son's request. Wouldn't you be? No doubt, the father probably denied him at first; however, the Bible doesn't say. This is a parable. Can you imagine how the father must have felt as he commanded the servants to saddle up the son's horse, watching them as they lay the spoils upon it? I imagine tears rolling down the father's face knowing that this decision could cost the child his very life. I'm of the opinion that the father, with loving words, whispered to his son concerning the pitfalls that were awaiting him. I can see the father pleading with him, asking him to wait, because it's better at home than out there.

Surely, his father can remember when he was once a young, impressionable boy. You know the same talk we have and our parents had with us about the wolves in sheep's clothing. Unfortunately, this generation feels they too, are entitled to have specific things simply because they were born. Not so! All were not born with a silver spoon in their mouths, and certain items are not a part of their well-being or part of their survival. Some are just spoiled by parents...mine were. The obligations of the parents are to feed, dress, shelter them, and provide them with the best education we can. We as saints must remind ourselves and our children not to give into peer pressure from circles of friends. This young man meditated on where he was going once he got "his" inheritance. He wanted to be the life of the party; he wanted to be where the lights were flashing and everything was "howdy, howdy." He knew he could not do certain things in the company of real saints, *oops*, I mean his father. Therefore, he thought to himself, "I'm going to go where I can do what I desire to do, away from my father." A mother was never mentioned.

As the story goes, the son went to a faraway country and got entangled with riotous living which included immoral escapades. He did not recognize that his inheritance was dwindling down. When the son looked up, his "friends" and money were gone and a famine arose in that land. He began to be in want; he had fallen. This leads me to believe that the inheritance he received was so great, that he kept the economy and the party going a long time. Once his inheritance had been consumed, the good times were no more and suddenly, a famine arose. He now found himself in a distressed position, hungry and without any monies. He was spent. The Bible goes on to say that the son made himself a citizen or became a resident of that land. Apparently, if you become like them or stay within that country, you could receive low income benefits, FIA (Family Independence Agency), WIC, (Women Infants and Children) Red Cross Assistance etc. This was a terrible life for a Jewish man. Don't misunderstand me: I am not putting those who need these services down; we must start from the bottom some times.

According to the Bible, the boy went to a faraway country. What this means for us is that we have walked away or we are far from God, our Father, and was/is lost. When we walk away from God, we sell our souls and our bodies to the highest bidder. The Bible says in Mark 8:36-37, *"what shall it profit a man to gain the whole world and lose his own soul? Or what shall he give in exchange for his soul?"* His Word also says this in Proverbs 14:12, *"there is a way which seemeth right unto a man, but the end thereof are the ways of death"*. This death is spiritual first, and then can become natural. Handle this: the funny thing is that the same company he spent his inheritance on treated him less than a servant. With friends like that, who needs enemies? I say this because the Bible says he got a job, slopping swine, and meals were not a part of the deal. He was on a hunger strike, involuntarily. Isn't it interesting how the same people you spend your money on, possibly help pay their rent and assist them with other concerns suddenly cannot not be found when you need them most? The Bible says that those people would not help him (Luke 15:16). *"And when he came to himself, he said, How many hired servants of my father's have bread enough and to spare, and I perish with hunger!"* (Luke 15:17). Father, will you take me back?

Beloved, as you read this book, you are searching for understanding on how to live a set apart life. You are already there or seeking to be there, which ever…the next paragraph will help you. I don't know where our heavenly Father has found you in your life. Whether it's in a hog pen or a drug den; it really doesn't matter. Because of His love, He will take us back after we've messed up over and over again. He will forgive us, reinstate us, cover us in His plan and put us back in heavenly places. Isn't it wonderful that the sovereign God receives our honest repentance, gives forgiveness after His heart has judged us, receiving us back home again?

He's the living God that will see us slipping slowly away from Him and will say, "Son or daughter, you're fading from me." What has your attention greater than Him? Now, if we continue to waver and straddle the fence, playing a hop scotch game with the world, He will remove the grace and allow the enemy to have his way with us. God's grace is sufficient; however, the Bible declares in Romans 6:1-2, *"What shall we say then? Shall we continue in sin, that grace may abound? God forbid. How shall we, that are dead to sin, live any longer therein?"* I believe with the right motives and instructions, you can live a fulfilled life free from bondage.

Come on back as the prodigal son did. Fall on your knees and ask the Father for His forgiveness. If you're reading this, it's not too late. He's patiently awaiting your return. Don't be as the friends of prodigal son. They'd come to church and get their "church on," leave really excited, but without a change of heart.

I must expose this truth about grave jumping that you may govern yourselves according to God's master plan. I once was you and did the exact same thing for years. I would just sit there, feeling guilty yet not wanting to commit to change. Because I said to myself, "Jesus and I have an understanding, and besides; I'm not ready to come back and *be* the church yet!" Whoa! Thank God for His mercy and grace; that was foolishness! I'm trying to help you!

I know you desire a better life for yourself and your family. However, you have not completed that life insurance application yet. Clearly, it's a policy that defines in the small lines that although you will lose your life to gain it, it is very beneficial for you and your family upon your death. The Bible describes the policy requirements as this in Mark 8:35: *"For whosoever will save his life shall lose it; but whosoever shall lose his life for my sake and the gospel's, the same shall save it"*. In Christ, you must take up your own cross and run your own salvation race. Many pretend to love Him and play games on Sunday, according to Matthew 15:8-9a: *"The people draweth nigh unto me with their mouth, and honoreth me with their lips; but their heart is far from me. But in vain they do worship me..."* God, our Father is a gentleman; He will not force His love and salvation on you. You must ask for a heart of flesh so He may penetrate your heart to repentance. If you do not have ears to hear at this moment, I want you to know you are being deceived.

Because most insurance companies sell more than one type of insurance, high pressure sales are not necessary. Most of them are patient and secure in the products that they are presenting to you. Dear loved one, I'm here to let you know the Father is reaching out to you at this moment because His Son paid a high premium for your life with His blood. Now is the time to check your spiritual retirement plan. You just might need to renew your policy. You might just need to upgrade and apply for the full package so you will be covered in all areas (*baptism, salvation, deliverance* and *healing*). I am not saying stop coming to the hospital (church) of hope. I am saying come to the hospital with an honest heart. I want to assure you as the man in the commercial assures you: you are in good "hands" with God. Don't stop coming to the altar; come with a made up mind to renew your salvation plan in Christ.

For all of those who have already repented or turned in the old insurance policy (fun now, eternal damnation later) for a new one (salvation in Jesus Christ), congratulations! Thank God you realized you needed a whole policy and not a term policy. From this point, with the right life insurance you are no longer living for the weekend, but living for the day

He will call you home. I want to jog your memory to remind you that we are aliens, a royal priesthood, chasing after the kingdom of God, its pleasures and the promise of everlasting life with the King of glory. We are passing through on our way home to be with the Father. If you are done with perpetrating a fraud Monday through Saturday with people who cannot care for your soul, keep reading. The Bible tells us to be separate from them. You are no longer your own; again, we've been bought with the blood of Jesus. We are to be bearers of excellence in Christ, because our lives will be the only Bible that some people will read.

Let me remind you of this: in order to receive the full benefit of your life insurance in Christ, you must first believe again in the deity of who God is…Jesus. What are you saying? I am relaying to you that the deity of Jesus Christ is one that believes in the Father, the Son and the Holy Ghost as one, and that Jesus is the Son of God. That same Son died on the cross and rose again with all power in His hands. You must believe that He, the Son, right now is sitting on the right side of the Father. Simply put, that Jesus is God. I realize I might be talking to some who are not sure how the Father is all three in one. If you would just humor me for a moment, I will give you an explanation in child-like understanding.

I am a mother, sister, cousin, entrepreneur, pastor and so on. I use those personalities when they are required and I never get those positions confused. Those personalities come out at its appointed time. However, I am only one person; that's just how the Father operates. He is *all* that we need and He never gets our needs and His roles confused, no matter who calls on Him. He has it all under control; yet, the Father is one God. Our Father wants us to know there is nothing out there in this world but heartache, headache, and pain. Although it may look delicious, at the end, hell you will gain. He wants us to know that with His policies, there is love, joy, and peace. He loves us with an everlasting love. Because He is that love, nothing can separate us from His love, no matter what we have done. The burial arrangements are already taken care of in Him. When we accept Him…we are buried with Him and we rise in Him!

You're probably saying, "I've already been there and it's too hard to live so *saved*." We've all been there. Please understand, by no means am I saying that it's easy; anything that's worth having isn't easy. The question then becomes, "How bad do you want it ... salvation?" God believes you were worth all the pain. Do you? He thinks you are and were; that's why He sent His Son. I know some days you will feel like throwing in the towel and say forget it; believe me I still have those days ... sometimes. Forgetting what I have to gain and living a life without fatherly holy restrictions, as a child with no boundaries. The Bible says in 1 Corinthians 13:11, "*When I was a child, I spake as a child...but when I became a man*, (not necessarily gender specific here), *I put away childish things*". Therefore, I declare that it is time to give up the reckless lifestyle, allow God to gather your broken pieces and mature in God. When you think about what He's already done and what didn't happen, it is good that you have an eternal life insurance policy (*salvation*) when this life is over.

I feel as Bishop David L. Ellis and his son, Bishop Charles H. Ellis would always say about certain things: "It's better to have it and not need it, than to need it and not have it." Some trials, tribulations and challenges concerning salvation cannot all be explained in one book. Some wisdom and understanding only come by living through it. Because baby, as the commercial from years ago stated "The proof is in the pudding." In other words, if you really want Jesus and the life He offers, the proof is in your saved-staying power. God needs to be your A, B, and C plan...*your* only plan.

God knows that we will be tested and tempted. The Bible says that *"a just man falleth seven times, and riseth up again..."* (Proverbs 24:16a). So, it's alright. Each time you fall, just don't stay there. We are likened unto a sheet of unshaped steel to a lathe engineer, who shapes steel for usage. When he wants to make a tool, he must first look for the perfect type of steel. Usually, a person would use a lathe and galvanized steel to form the tool he desires to make. After he forms the tool, he must harden it by putting it in a furnace, leaving it in approximately 30-45 minutes depending on the type of work you plan to use it for.

Catch everything I'm saying now. When

you take out the steel, you must clean it off with sandpaper or a hard bristle brush; the pressure on the steel again will depend upon how you plan to use it. The lathe worker puts the steel back in the furnace again to burn off the unusable parts. Once it's out, you sand again. Once the tool is smooth, it is perfect for usage and unbreakable, no matter what the weather or condition of the work.

Does this sound familiar? The Father does the same things with us, if we let Him. He's the lathe expert and we are the imperfect sheet of steel. He bends us, stretches us in all situations that we may be pliable and able to withstand the devil in the evil days. He also puts us in the fire that when we are cured, He pulls us out and we are ready to be used. He's calling for holiness and sanctification; there's no other way. You've lost your way, but that's rectifiable. Repent and come back home; He's standing and waiting with an outstretched hand.

The Bible says that after the son critiqued his behavior and attitude, he came to himself, turned with a repenting heart, and started for home. His father saw him afar off and he received him with the same love he left. The Bible says he called for the others, including the servant; because his son was coming home. The son began to repent, and tell of his wrong; he was new in His heart. The Bible declares that *"...if any man be in Christ, he is a new creature; old things are passed away; behold, all things are become new* (2 Corinthians 5:17). The son had humbled himself and wanted to be a servant, but the father did not allow this; the father restored him back into the same place in the palace as before. The Bible states that the father told his servant to put a robe on the son, which showed restoration (*covering/ honor/redemption*), sandals on his feet (*a sign of no longer a slave/servant to what he had been bound to. Because servants did not wear shoes, he had no balance; shoes stabilizes our walk and give us grip to stand*) and his ring (*restored inheritance/authority/son-ship*). This tells me that when the son returned home, he no longer looked of royalty, but had the look of a lost soul. The son was barren and empty. We have all been there, lost like a ship without a sail.

Oftentimes, we come to God the same way, all spiritually broken, and in need of a break through. Aren't you glad that Jesus is our stabilizer? Just as the natural father restores, so will your heavenly Father restore you back to your rightful place. He is a restorer of all, and if you've never called on Him for your whole life insurance plan…its time.

My friend, I am not saying that all your problems will magically disappear; of course they won't. But all issues are better with Him than without Him. The grass always looks greener on the other side, but after the sun hides its face, you realize it's all burned up. Let me remind you of one last story. In Luke 15:4, there was a man who had a hundred sheep and one got away. Although the Bible doesn't say this, but I'm sure the man felt heartbroken; he had given the sheep everything it needed to survive and yet, the sheep allowed something to lure him away from his fathers' care. *The man decided he would leave the 99 sheep and go look for the one sheep that walked away.* He knew that life with him for the sheep was better than being out in the wilderness fully exposed to all manner of things that could harm or even kill the sheep. When the man found his sheep, I can see him dusting the sheep off. The sheep was probably filthy, a little maimed, bruised and worn out from its travels. The man put the sheep on his shoulders to carry him home. The man got the sheep home, washed him, gave him food, and then laid him on a bed of warm hay. Afterwards, *the man called his friends and family to celebrate the return of his lost sheep. It goes on to say that there will be more joy in heaven over one sinner who repents than over ninety-nine just persons who needs no repentance.* The Father and the angels are anticipating your return.

Are you separated from God today? There is a way out. Isaiah 59:1-2 says *"Behold, the Lord's hand is not shortened, that it cannot save, nor His ear heavy that it cannot hear: but your iniquities have separated you from your God, and your sins have hid His face from you, that He will not hear"*. I am not encouraging or supporting a particular Christian organization. I wish to introduce you to the Savior, and His name is Jesus. We are in the last days, folks. We don't know the hour or the day our Father will return. We don't know when our souls will be required of us; but one thing is for sure: He's coming back with a reward in His hand.

Remember beloved, 2 Peter 3:9 states that

"The Lord is not slack concerning His promise, as some count slackness, but is longsuffering to us-ward, not willing that any should perish, but that all should come to repentance". Amen.

Beloved, if you're ready to return to the Father and you do not have your Bible with you, here's a prayer of repentance that you can say with your heart and your lips. You can repeat this anywhere: your workplace, in the airport, at the bus station, even in the grocery store. God can hear you speaking softly to Him. Therefore, my friends, if you haven't gotten your eternal insurance policy yet, there is a basic repentance membership quote below to start you on the road to recovery. Are you ready to get restored back into your Father's house? Then repeat this prayer: *Father, in the name of Jesus; I come humbly to the throne of grace. First, I thank You for your grace and mercy, your love, and my life today. Father, because I do believe that Jesus is your Son whom You raised from the dead; and that only in His name by grace through faith can salvation be received. I ask for forgiveness for my sins of commission and sins of omission. I recognize that I am a man or woman with unclean lips, unclean heart and unclean thoughts. I ask that*

You come into my heart by your spirit. Be my Lord and Savior and restore my soul. I thank You Jesus for my new life and a relationship with the Father in Jesus' name, Amen. Remember, this is your life, *After the Alter.* Amen.

3

A FAITHLESS GENERATION

Faith is, as the Bible tells us in Hebrew 11:1, 3, *"Now faith is the substance of things hoped for, the evidence of things not seen...Through faith we understand that the worlds were framed by the word of God, so that things which are seen were not made of things which do appear"*. It also tells us that *faith without works is dead.*

I remember hearing faith messages growing up in church, and the pastors making this statement, "Faith without works is dead." I thought to myself, *"Okay, there's got to be more to this thing."* As I sought the Father for myself, continued to grow spiritually in the Word of God and was no longer just a "pew warmer," He revealed so many things to me over these 25 years. Now, I understand better what it means to have strong faith through trials and tribulations. I've learned how to use my faith to mentally get through sexual violations during my childhood and even as an adult. Most of all,

I used faith to receive His love and His salvation. This faith walk is every day and it is putting off old thinking, no longer trusting in material things and beginning to exchange those thoughts into what God desires me to think. It became a lifestyle. Faith is the thing that carries you from day to day, hope to hope, and from glory to glory in God. It takes faith to receive His salvation and His spirit. He has given us all a measure of faith to build from, as a grain of a mustard seed.

Let's pause right here at the "mustard seed" concept. Have you ever wondered why the Lord would use such a small seed to demonstrate the amount of faith needed to receive the manifestation from requests made unto Him? In Luke 17:6, Jesus said, *"...If you have the faith as a grain of mustard seed, ye might say to this sycamine tree, 'Be thou plucked up by the root, and be thou planted in the sea'; and it should obey you."* After an in-depth research on the mustard seed, it came to me that as people of God, some of us might not realize how fast the mustard seed plant actually grows. I wonder how many of us have taken the time to learn just how potent that little seed really is. It is ingenious how the Father used the mustard seed to illustrate how quickly our faith can grow in the correct spiritual soil. Earlier in this chapter, I said that the Father, by faith, framed the worlds. The worlds in this sense means shaped the ages of time. He spoke it and it came into existence. The Word of God tells us that the earth is the Lords and the fullness thereof, and they that dwell therein. Therefore, I pondered why God speaking the worlds into existence was mentioned. As I continued to inquire of the Lord, He let me know that information was written for us.

The Father wanted us to know that because faith is a part of our kingdom birth inheritance, we have the power to speak a thing into existence, in this age…this world. However, the catalyst is that we must speak or pray His will and then He shall perform it, by faith in Jesus' name. And just in case you are one of those people who used tears for fears, the Father is not moved by tears alone. You must have some faith to go along with those tears. I know His Word says in Psalms 56:8 that He bottles up those tears and remembers them. He does, however, there is a kingdom law that must be accomplished by those tears; faith. He is also not moved by anger, pride, foolery, but by faith, then your tears.

I am reminded of the story of Samuels' mother, Hannah, which is found in the first chapter of 1 Samuel. Hannah was barren and because of that, the Bible says that her heart was heavy (paraphrasing) and she cried daily. I can imagine that she must have cried for years and years, and yet, did not conceive. The Bible says that her husband's other wife, Peninnah, had children, Hannah did not. This led me to believe while studying, that there were several years of sorrow, envy, and disappointment. Elkanah, her husband, could not give Hannah anything for her grief. Not one pearl, diamond, land or home; she was barren and childless! Now hear this: through the many years of suffering and anguish in silence, Hannah did not move God, until she showed an act of faith. She put movement (as we say in Christendom) to her faith.

First, Hannah got up after her husband sacrificed to God and crawled up the stairs (movement, act of faith) into the tabernacle to pray for herself. She didn't stand in the prayer line at church and ask someone else to pray for her; she prayed for herself (there's nothing wrong with prayer lines). She didn't call the pastor to fast with her or call the intercessors to intercede on her behalf. She used her own faith and prayed *for* herself. Secondly, she was so filled with grief that the priest thought she was drunk because there was movement of her lips, but, no words were heard. Again, she was grieved and she *was* barren. Hannah worked her faith by speaking to her situation. She told the priest that she *poured out her heart unto the Lord and had not* (catch this) *spoken it until now* (made her petition known) *unto the Lord."* The Bible says in 1 Samuel 1:17, which you can read the complete text during your studies, that Eli (the priest) said to her, *"Go in peace, and the God of Israel grant your petition which you have asked* (spoken) *of Him.* I believe there was a praise that took place after that. Thirdly, the Bible says *"she went her way and ate, and her face was no longer sad."*

Do you understand what I have written thus far? It's a faith walk. The Bible states clearly that you must believe you have received that which you are asking before you can see it. The scripture, *"walking by faith and not by sight"* yells seeing it before you see it and being a prophet of your own destiny. *Now faith is…* the substance of things hoped for, the evidence of things not seen. The faith of hope undergirds or supports your belief in the thing you're waiting for. Put works with your faith as Hannah did and watch the substance of things hoped for and evidence of things not seen show up! The word "works" is a verb. Thus, action is required. Movement, some kind of participation on our behalf is required. We must give God something to work with. You will see that statement again in this book. We exchange our faith for the thing we hope to see and or accomplish. We exchange our hope for salvation, peace, healing, etc. We lift our faith cup up to God as an offering. Check your faith receptacle!

In the Word of God, whenever someone went to the Father in prayer in the Old Testament or New Testament, God would always ask something of them in return. Check the scriptures. You want from Him, and He wants from you! He doesn't need you to qualify Him as God; He needs your participation to be the God of your life. I'm talking about a faith walk. I am reminded of a time in 2009 when I was purchasing a home. I was short on the closing cost with only two days before closing. I remember praying and God did not answer. As I lay on my couch the day before, a small still voice spoke these words to me, "You must participate in your own miracle. A miracle takes place on the way to doing. A miracle happens while on the road of obedience." I said to the Father, "What?" The Spirit of God said, "You must participate in your own miracle." In John 5:6, 8, Jesus asked the lame man, *"Wilt thou be made whole?"...* Then *"Rise, take up they bed, and walk."* I was still a little dumbfounded by this. He whispered again, "If you ask them, I will cause a spirit of giving to come upon them and bless you." I jumped up, got on the telephone and began to cause the spirit of faith and telemarketing to work. I got all the money we needed in one day. Not only did I receive the closing cost, but I got enough money to pay for the house in cash. Hope did not change my circumstance alone; faith did.

Therefore, the *now* faith is that faith that should be working "right now," from the day that you and I heard His voice to come out of darkness into His marvelous light. We used faith for that and that's the faith that needs to grow. The work of faith will work if you understand how to work it. As I studied the Word of God, and the Spirit of God open up the spirit of understanding to write on this area of faith, He began to say, "For it is written in Romans 12:3b, that "...*God have dealt to every man the measure of faith*". As you believe, the more your faith-this faith will grow. It will grow into faith to be saved, faith to be sanctified, and faith to believe and live according to His commandments" and so on.

Let's be clear, He has given faith to all mankind; now, what you use it for is your choice. We have the same power that Jesus has; if we work it, if we believe it. We didn't earn it or buy it, we were born with it. It's ours to work the plan of prosperity for our lives in Christ. See it with me. The Father let me know that there are two ways to prosper: in peace or in fear. There is a price to be paid for both. Consequently, if we prosper by Him, we not only receive earthly blessings, but we'll gain eternal treasures in heaven. The unsaved is not so; they will pay with their lives to Hades to live in eternal damnation with *their* god.

Now, the Father is not against His children having nice things including finances; even Jesus had a treasurer for necessities, but remember His Word in Matthew 6:33 reminds us to *"Seek ye first the kingdom of God and His righteousness; and all these things shall be added unto you"*. He is instructing us to follow our manuals for longevity to a healthy and prosperous life. It's in the book! You need to know that all of those things above are done by faith. The unsaved may prosper, but, to whom did they sell their soul to get it? When this life is over, will they burn or will they rejoice?

Let's look further as the Father has shared a few mysteries with me. I'll pay it forward by sharing them with you. The world says it like this: "You must put in sweat equity." When you're employed, if you want a pay check at the end of the week, you must obey the rules of sweat equity. So, in God, you must work the principles of faith equity; if you put it in, you shall receive your reward at pay day. It works according to the power that works in you.

Let's continue. Genesis 1:26a says *"Let us*

make man in our own image" (with everything He has, including power and anointing) we have it. The scam artist, the hustler and even the dancer knows that if they put their faith into action (works), they will receive what they desire in their heart (hope) because they put into action the vision in their minds, and brought it to pass through works-money!

People of God, laziness profits nothing, faith gains much. The Bible tells us in Proverbs 13:4, *"The soul of the sluggard desireth, and hath nothing: but the soul of the diligent shall be made fat"*. We want blessings without having faith and no work just because we're saved. Don't fool yourselves; it won't work. You must give the Father something to work with. For without faith, it is impossible to please God. If we desire to please Him, then we must give back what He gave us-faith. He sees it and then blesses us. In the body, we expect God to do it. There's an old song entitled *God Bless the Child* by the late great Billie Holiday, a blues singer. In that song, she sang, "God bless the child that's got his own." What?

That means God blesses the child who has *his own* tenacity and faith to make something happen in this world. By faith, *you can do all things through Christ which strengthens you* (Philippians 4:13) as you trust Him while living the Bible out loud. We should not expect God to do what we can do in our own strength.

We depend on Him to do what's impossible for us to do. A father does not repeatedly put worms on the end of a fishing rod after showing his son how to do it; he can do it for himself. Now, the world will use their measure of faith by putting it to work. They move their desires into existence with an "I got this" mentality. Whether it's for finances, houses, cars, or whatever: understand equitably that faith will work, if you work it.

We, as the body, should be embarrassed that the world applies the Word of God better than we do. They use it to gain the things of this world. I know we are aliens, waiting on our real home to show up. However, on this journey we should acquire spiritual things and some natural possessions along the way. If we do it God's way, you and I can have those things to enjoy and then receive our just reward from our heavenly Father as well. He says that we can have things, just do not allow these things to absorb or *have* us. In other words, don't allow the love of money or the love of earthly possessions to distract you, my friend. This will obstruct our view of Him.

There was a book written on the law of attraction. This book is filled with New Ageism, mysticism, and philosophies along with a few biblical principles sprinkled on top to draw us in. I am not saying the Bible is the only thing we should read; I am simply saying that you must discern (take notice) when to shut out all the other voices in your head and adhere only to one voice; God's. The Bible says that His children hear his voice, and He knows them, and they will follow Him. (John 10:27). Plainly put, you cannot chase and listen to every voice that sounds good. For those of you with itchy ears, running around listening to every voice (I won't be specific, not to defend) to hear this preacher and that preacher preach about this and that: settle yourself down and sit down first the master teacher (God) so you can *hear* correctly. Although I am a pastor/preacher, I want you to study so that when you hear me share the word, you will know if it's that truth (gospel) that makes one free!

We, the Body of Christ, have a best seller's book, the Bible. But, did you know that the Bible fell to number two as the highest sold book next to the book, *The Secret*. Why? Because unfortunately, many of us were reading that book to find out the "secret" instead of reading the Bible. Incredibly, I am guessing that although they read it, only a small percentage of those people are actually in a different and/or better place than they were before they read the book. Why? Because, it doesn't matter what you settle yourself to read; if you don't apply the principles, the plan will not work.

This book says put your faith into works and think, not speak, things into existence, and those thoughts will attract what you want. Hear me; I am not saying that the writer is wrong. Remember, I said the book is dusted with a few Biblical principles. Let us not forget that the kingdom of God is a system. He has already given us a blueprint, its own law of attraction, so that we don't bailout or take flight when hardship comes. Hardship will come; believe me. He says in His Word, if we ask for wisdom, He will give it to us liberally; freely (James 1:5).

He is a supplier who promises to supply all our needs. However, all things come by the law of faith. God will show us how to have faith to be healed, faith to prosper, faith to be delivered, faith to receive employment, etc. All these things come by faith. It will continue to work as long as you're building those faith muscles. I hope I made this plain; a good mother doesn't put a meal on the countertop where her three-year-old child can't see it, but she puts it on the baby table where the child can reach and partake of it.

When we walk in faith, it shows itself outwardly. It tells a dying world that our hope is built on nothing less, than Jesus' blood and righteousness. Remember, God has gifted us *all* with a measure of faith. Use the gift that the Father has given you to build on your most holy faith. If you're still having a problem with faith and there seems to be more doubt, began to exercise those faith muscles. Start with a small request first, and build from there. Train your heart to believe by getting faith scriptures and meditating on them day and night.

Now, I need to go backwards a little. I must finish discussing the mustard seed faith and doubt. Doubt can be snuffed out with daily meditation, communication with God and with that mustard seed of faith. I know it's hard to walk in faith when the inner man, your enemy, is fighting with you to do things the old way...your way.

Let's look into the anatomy of the mustard seed. The mustard seed plant is approximately 1.2 millimeters and, like your faith, it is not seen until it has been tried in the fire a few times. If the seeds are allowed to mature on the plant, they will grow and continue to provide plenty for mustard making. The mustard seed has the ability to grow into a mighty plant that produces offspring in great abundance. The seed (your faith) produces growth in as little as 30-60 days depending on the climate (the pressure you're under). This seed has a reputation of having great piquancy, and is supported by numerous passages found everywhere from the Bible to Shakespeare.

Can we discuss this deeper? The mustard seed (your faith) has the ability to grow in great abundance (to believe God for anything). Your faith piquancy (strong belief system in God) is supported by the many testimonies given by you and others you come in contact with. A mustard seed is known for its strength (rooted faith) and ability to produce oil (anointing on your life, which cannot be hidden). However, strangely enough, it contains no cholesterol (imbalance or carnality), only a small trace of vegetable fat (doubt), and then protein (prayer), calcium (fasting), and other ingredients (fellowship with the Father, praise, worship, and the consistent gathering with the saints, etc.). Once the seed becomes a tree (rooted, unmovable), it can grow up to 15 feet (easily seen) with a thick main stem (unbreakable) and branches strong enough to bear the weight of a bird (can handle adversity with ease). This, ladies and gentlemen, is faith. This is what Gods' eyes roam the earth to find in this generation. Now…faith is the substance, the desire, the hoped for, and the goal that you seek after to please Him. God is faithful, yes! So put your trust in Him, who created you, that He may cultivate the faith in you.

As I close this chapter, understand that we use the gift of faith to live the Bible out loud. I want to leave you with these thoughts. As God framed the world with His words, we must frame our lives with the Word and the faith God has given to us. If we learn to use our faith as God did in the beginning, we will be unstoppable against the enemy. The Bible says it like this in Romans 10:17: *"So then faith cometh by hearing and hearing by the word of God"*. I am expressing to you that faith comes by hearing, and hearing by the word of God. Repetition is the key. Please do not forget that in this salvation walk, you will need to make a choice: you are going to live by faith or you are going to live *in* fear. Both will challenge you in the way you live your life. Both will confront you in how you will live the Bible out loud. God, in His mercy and love, gives us a choice in this life whether we will live as a saint or sinner. I suggest you choose life and that more abundantly. The devil will be after you with everything he's got when you walk *boldly* in faith. Some days your faith muscles will need to be exercised more than others. But, bear in mind my friend, that faith does show your integrity to God and His integrity to you. You must walk in it to become it. Faith strengthens your anointing in God, *After the Alter*. Amen.

4

PEOPLE OF WAR

In the armed forces, when a mission comes about, the joint chief of staff must communicate plainly to others concerning strategic tactics and the threats that will be encountered upon entering enemy territory. Oftentimes, before an enemy strikes, there are warnings that the enemy may send. It is generally up to Congress if they will heed to the warning and what the retaliation will be. In all armed forces, their strategies come from knowing their enemy; there is a protocol that cannot be deviated from. Victory depends on the accuracy and efficiency of this protocol. When an attack is at hand, soldiers must be briefed on the target before entering the battlefield. This is to ensure smooth and precise execution when fighting with the proper weapons. The proper weapons include proper clothing, the soldier's combat uniform; which includes headgear and footwear. Along with their dress, they must obtain the right weapons to defeat the enemy. No one is thinking of retreating unless there is a command given from the commanding officer(s). They must put on their war faces, and be in the right mindset for battle and warfare. It's strategic and it's all or nothing!

Can we consider your local police department? When there is a raid on a suspected drug house or a prostitution ring, it's no holds barred. There is much preparation that takes place before the raid can happen. The police force knows their enemy; they have done an in-depth investigation on the perpetrator, the subject who is usually suspected of a certain crime. Like the armed forces, they also must be dressed for the task. Although there is a saying that there are always casualties of war, the officers always hope for the best. In their minds, it's only about getting the enemy under their feet and in their control in order to apprehend them. That's the goal! What do these two forces have in common? *Strategy*. Oftentimes, good strategy will allow you to prevail in a task.

When considering the mind of a strategist. I would be remiss if I did not mention one of the most prominent boxing champions known in the world: Cassius Marcellus Clay, Jr. a.k.a. the great Muhammad Ali. Here's something I learned from watching old videos as well as reading about him as a young girl. The champ would begin the fight mentally, even before his opponents stepped foot into the ring. Ali would brag intensely about how he was too fast for his opponent to keep up with him. Typically, Ali would set up the poor chap with media harassment, taunting, mind games etc., for weeks on end before a fight; sometimes even years. He did this with great expectation to weaken them. He would casually bully an opponent by predicting which round he would knock them out. The press would gobble this up, specifically, Howard Cosell. Ali's speed and the way he opened a fight with a flurry of dancing and feet skipping moves to tire out his opponent made them nervous and rendered Ali most feared, to say the least. He would watch, patiently waiting for fatigue to set in on his opponent. Once fatigue would overcome his opponent, thereafter the blows would come; Ali was ruthless. A left then a right; a jab here, a jab there! He'd take the opportunity to pounce on his opponent as a lion on sheep; backing him into the corner of the ring. There they were dangling by the ropes, punch after punch after punch. Muhammad Ali, a boxing strategist.

And for you basketball fans, here's a little something for you. Michael Jordan used similar tactics as Muhammad Ali in his phenomenal career. What do these athletes have in common? Mind Games. You'll see that title again. Once Michael Jordan was able to get inside his competitor's head from all the sports bullying and finally meet face to face on the "wood," the game is most likely already won, because of fear. Michael Jordan was one of the most feared players in the NBA, from the front office to the court. If he was happy, he put the butts in the seats and a "W" was imminent. If he was unhappy, he would still put the butts in the seats. However, you did not want to deal with his monstrous rage during and after the games. He was competitive. He was powerful on and off the court. From here, my point begins.

God never promised us that we would not go through the valley of the shadow of death; He promised that He will never leave us nor forsake us as we go; for you must remember that it's only the shadow of death, not death itself. God lets us know in His Word that we are doing just that; *going through it* (Psalms 23:4). He also conveys to us that the enemy will come to battle with us, but it is not ours, but His (2 Chronicles 20:15). Now, if we lean and depend on Him, we win. In Deuteronomy 31:6, the Father reminds us to *be strong and courageous and know that he is with us, and he will never leave us.* Though we know that the battle isn't ours, we still must dress for the fight. Dressing for this battle starts with prayer. Philippians 4:6a tells us to *"Be careful for nothing; but in everything by prayer and supplication"*.

What is prayer? Well, prayer is communication with God and His communication with you. You cannot take prayer outside of the realm of the kingdom. In other words, you must pray to the King on His terms by using kingdom principles to reach Him. You must know the right codes to reach the heavens and know where these codes are located. Where are they located? Sunday School Class 101…the Bible. The code is praying scripture back unto the Lord. If we use these instructions accurately with faith, beginning with *acknowledging the Lord in all our ways* (Proverbs 3:6), we will surely move the heavens. We'll use the Word of God to destroy the plans and plots of our enemy and we will have direct insight. This is the first strategy to winning the battle; having entail on your enemy by the Holy Spirit.

In the Bible days, when the men went to war, they needed to be dressed properly for war. To me, they seemed to be in war all the time. Let's begin with their headgear. The soldiers wore a bronze helmet which had leather straps (to keep it from falling off). It also covered the back of their necks to protect them from neck injuries, death by head roll and extreme sunburn. Secondly, the breastplate covered the men from their chest area down to their thighs, which was made of bronze as well. Thirdly, there was a wide belt that covered the waist line which was equipped with first aid supplies for injuries. Fourthly, they carried large shields. This shield was long and oval shaped with two layers of wood covered with linen or animal hide bound together with iron soaked in water (this shielded them from the fiery darts). On his legs, he wore bronze greaves and a bronze javelin was slung on his back. The soldiers also carried a short two-edged sword, which was very powerful, not because it was sharp but because it was used to attack at close range. Oftentimes, you would not see it coming. Lastly, the soldiers wore sandals with cleats made of sharp nails designed to give firm footing on rough surfaces. Again, all of these things must be in place in hopes to have victory over their enemy.

Well, my brothers and sisters, as in the world, so in the spirit; we have been called to war. We must have our spiritual war clothes on by *having on the whole armor of God,* Ephesians 6:12. We must have our armor on for battle, and our feet pointed toward heaven. How do we defeat the devil? How do we get the upper hand as soldiers for Christ, as the earlier saints who have gone on before us? The answer is by prayer and fasting. We need to have our prayer game firm. Although we know that the fight is *already* fixed, we need to bring it from the spiritual to manifestation by prayer. By prayer, the Father is able to disclose the devil's weapons before they get a chance to land. We can only do this by communicating with the Father as the commanding chief must do with his soldiers. The Word of God tells us that the Father *will reveal mysteries unto us* (Daniel 2:22).

However, there must be a relationship with the Father, which starts with having a prayer life. Prayer is mentioned or referenced over 400 times in the Bible. I believe God had a lot to say about communicating with Him, whether this was by mentioning it or showing it through the Psalms and other Scriptures. Prayer is major in God's eyes.

There's a power that comes when your prayer life is coupled by fasting. Your fasting is substantiated by prayer and your prayer life is substantiated with faith; it is a threefold cord. If you pray, it is written in the Bible that you have the power *to call those things that be not as though they were* (Romans 4:17). We *can speak to the mountain and it* (the situation, issue, problem, thing, illness, etc.) *must move* (Mark 11:23). But these are just to name a few things when you have a prayer life (i.e. communication with the Father). Romans 8:14, 26-27 says:

"For as many are led by the spirit of God, they are the sons of God. Likewise, the Spirit also helpeth our infirmities: for we know not what we should pray for as we ought: but the Spirit itself maketh intercession for us with groanings which cannot be uttered. And he that searcheth the

hearts knoweth the mind of the Spirit, because he maketh intercession for the saints according to the will of God".

When you have the Holy Spirit (God) living within you, this connects you to the Father, it will begin to pray for you in the spirit; thereby causing you to speak in your heavenly language (tongues) to get what's on God's mind. While that occurs, the Spirit of God will spiritually reveal mysteries to you so you can pray it outwardly and into the atmosphere, keeping you from praying amiss (against a moving target).

Praying is not just so you can talk to God, but so the Father can talk back to you. In the beginning, the Father again demonstrated how important communication is. In Genesis 1, the Father spoke the earth into existence. God said, *"Let there be,"* and it was. And God said, *"Let the waters under the heaven be gathered together unto one place, and let the dry land appear,"* and it did…communication. As we continue to commune with the Father through prayer, you may find that you have the gift of an intercessor (baring the burdens of others when you pray).

An intercessor can feel the pressures of life and as the Father reveals mysteries in prayer by His Holy Spirit, you will begin to pray as accordingly to God's will. I want to mention right here that a consistent prayer life will shift your prayer direction and take you into higher realms of the spirit in God. The *moaning and groaning that cannot be uttered* (Romans 8:26) will begin to take on a life of its own; it'll sound different each time you pray and go deeper in God (closer walk with Him). Let's take it up for understanding.

Most women in labor will always make a loud grunting sound right before the baby's head begins to crown (break forth out of the vaginal area). Although she has made sounds during the complete labor process, this sound of birthing is different and even more painful than she'd ever imagined. Each time you pray, you're setting yourself up in the birthing position. Therefore, manifestation is the result of prayer and there should always be a sound of praise before and after. So beloved, as you read this book and learn more about prayer, make the sound of praise and worship before prayer, giving the Father praise from your heart. Let your praise reflect your expectations from the Father. Because of your prayers by faith, God shall break bondages off your life and continuously release peace upon you.

Also, because of your worship after and before prayer, you create a sweet aroma unto God which creates an atmosphere for the Father to enter into where you are. Now, at this moment I want to remind you that prayer won't always change your situation; but God will change you in the midst of your situation, when your heart is filled with faith. His Word becomes fulfilled in your life. Build Him an altar of prayer, praise and worship right in the midst of your growing up in Him; and you too, shall be *victorious*. There's power in prayer, there is power in fasting, there's power in praise, there's power in your true worship, and most importantly, there's power in His blood.

I must also tell you that the spiritual climate in your life will began to change for a few reasons. For one, in simple terms, you have decided to partake in your inheritance… receiving salvation. You are reading the Bible and understand, hopefully by now just how powerful *you* are! The enemy is now on high alert because he lost another one, and that joker will come after you. The process of following the rules of engagement is *working out your own salvation with fear and trembling* (Philippians 2:12).

After the Alter, the metamorphosis of you will begin as you learn to live the Bible out loud. Living the Bible out loud starts with laying a good foundation and prayer does that. When a foundation starts with high quality, the building (us) that sits on it will be well, sturdy, unmovable, non-wavering and balanced. We are soldiers of war; therefore, we need to entreat our Commander in Chief, Jesus. Nothing should be done without seeking counsel from our Lord and Savior. Yes, God can speak through others. However, when God speaks to you, that word is not an opinion; it is straight from God's throne, spoken from God, Himself!

Once again, Satan will be after you because you are being armed with information vital to your new role, your recovery, and your victory through Christ Jesus. You will constantly be in a faith fight. But, it's worth it! Our Father in heaven is a strategist, much like when you play the game of chess. When you make a move to obey in faith, He will make a move to bless and restore, that you may recover all. When studying the Word, you will find that whenever the men of God would pray after an enemy strike, they asked if they could pursue. The Father would answer them when the enemy was at their weakest point (as do soldiers and athletes) instructing the men of God to pursue and recover the spoils. Whether you are a new convert or seasoned saint, you must adamantly pursue intimacy (communication, relationship) with the Father. Please understand that whenever we go in to pray, whether we're kneeling, standing, bending, lying prostrate, etc., the enemy is immediately at his weakest. He is no match against the power that's within us. *We are more than conquerors through him that loved us* (Romans 8:37), him being Christ Jesus.

If at this moment you're thinking, *I do enough praying,* that tells me you're not doing enough praying. We all can improve in that area. The Bible prompts us *to pray without ceasing* (1 Thessalonians 5:17) and *that men should always pray and not faint* (Luke 18:1). As you should know, there is always room for improvement.

You must have a teachable spirit, my dear, to grow in this walk. God teaches us through prayer and His written Word. That's why it's imperative that we pray daily. It doesn't always need to be a long prayer, but a powerful prayer. God does not look at the length of our prayer, but the length of our love and sincerity of heart. God is not always interested in the quantity, but the quality of our prayers. Understand, the more you seek after God, the more you will locate yourself. The more you chase God, the more you will understand your purpose. The more you seek after God, the more you will know Him and hear His voice.

When Satan begins to speak folly in your ear, which he will; what do you do? You plead the blood and speak the Word against him, that's your weapon. It is written, *"For the weapons of our warfare are not carnal, but mighty through God to the pulling down of strongholds"* (2 Corinthians 10:4). Assuredly, if Satan spoke to Jesus and tried to tempt Him to commit suicide, surely he will talk to us because we have God's spirit. Please understand that, Satan does talk. He impresses upon our minds; God impresses upon our spirit. Don't believe this falsehood going around that says "he does not talk and that it's all in your mind." Please know that they're absolutely right. It is all in your head, where your mind is. Again, the mind really is a battlefield!

A strong and guarded prayer and fasting life is essential to your salvation. It is the very essence of what stands between the spiritual and the natural, between life and death. Without prayer, we are infertile. Our spiritual womb is barren, (that's another book). As a woman who outwardly comes across as being physically healthy, but, after several years of trying to conceive a baby, finds that although she appeared to be well on the outside; inwardly, she is barren. Her womb does not store the strength it needs to carry a child full term and/or carry a child at all. She does not have the ability to be fruitful and multiply. In most cases, she will always miscarry. Don't miscarry or abort your purpose!

When it comes to praying and fasting, you must have the Word of God stored in you to fight. This gives you spiritual strength so you can communicate to God, praying His Word back to Him out of your spirit. When there is no communication with the Father, you have no strength to fight the devil in prayer. Also, just as a side note, fasting makes you more sensitive to the voice of God because you are denying yourself of fleshly desires, that you may hear God's voice. Fasting is a strategy as well. Surround yourselves with others who have a strong prayer and fasting lifestyle. The Bible declares that *"the effectual fervent prayer of a righteous man availeth much"*. (James 5:16).

Sometimes in this walk, we will need to radio for help to get us off the battlefield of life because, we too, can get wounded. Sometimes, we will need others to rescue us and pray for us until we are ready to fight again with all our hearts. Sometimes, there is a "man down" circumstance depending on how long you've been in a war with the devil. The Bible also admonishes us in that same passage *to pray for one another*. We will often need our brother and sister soldiers to gear up, stand up and help us fight through prayer. We don't always have the proper spiritual strength to defeat him. Yes, we know the correct prayer lingo because we hear people pray and know what to say around true intercessors. However, if you don't war in praying and fasting on your own; you will not bear warfare fruit and the devil will snipe you off. You will be weak to his devices. Salvation will continue to be in tact; but your fighting skills will be miniscule at best.

Outwardly, we can appear to be spiritually healthy; however, we are spiritually barren. Our prayers are fruitless and powerless due to our lack of communication with God. When we don't have the strength, the power of prayer in us, we, you, as babes in Christ, are often miscarried and lost back into the world. Once we have received His salvation, we must activate His power by communicating through a prayer and fasting relationship to defeat our enemy. I hope this makes sense. Miscarriage happens because we are not protecting the baby (communication/relationship with God). We must pray to allow our prayer life to grow properly (connecting with the correct spiritual nutrients) that it may produce good fruit.

It is a misnomer that because we attend church on Sundays, Tuesdays or whenever, that our lives are bearing the right fruit. In Galatians 5:22-23, *love, joy, peace, forbearance, kindness, goodness, faithfulness, gentleness and self-control;*

now that's a big one. These fruit are very important in our lives to maintain connection-relationship with God. We attend every public prayer meeting and yet, we still don't have a private prayer life. We attend every prayer conference and still don't have a prayer life or are bearing fruit; something must change. We attend every Bible study, and yet still don't have a prayer and fasting life. This entire thing means nothing if you don't have the power of God working and moving through you to produce victory in your life. We often substitute a private prayer life with a public prayer life so we can be seen by men. Guess what? God sees and knows our works. An anointed man or woman of God can discern the lack of power in your life when there is no movement when you pray. Come out of the closet, you closet saint! Repent and start again. Stop faking it! New convert, don't allow this to be named among you. Seasoned church member, locate yourself and see if this applies to you. We all need to do self-examination of the fruit we are bearing; we may have some rotten pieces and need God to prune.

I am reminded of the Scriptures in Mark

11:12-25, when Jesus was walking with His disciples, He observed a fig tree that should have produced fruit due to the season it was in. Now, although the tree had green leaves, once Jesus took a closer look, He noticed that underneath those green leaves, there were no figs. No *fruit* had been bored. The tree was barren. It had a look of fruitfulness, but had denied Jesus of that fruit due to its barrenness. If we don't have a consistent prayer life, the enemy will rob us of bearing good fruit in our lives. Please understand; you will bear fruit because we live in the flesh; but what type of fruit will it be? I am saying again: that we can appear to look like that of a prayer warrior, but truthfully, our prayer tree is barren when God looks upon us. The Bible states it like this: *having a form of godliness, but denying the power thereof* (2 Timothy 3:5). Be fruitful and multiply; this only happens through prayer. We are *powerless* without it! When prayer is strong, you can pray prophetically and stop the assignments of the enemy. Prayer is mentioned over and over and shown over and over again in the Bible.

While fasting is mentioned only 22 times,

both are important for spiritual growth. Your prayers do not need to be deep and long, you can just get to the point; God doesn't mind. My prayers and your prayers will not, and should not, mimic any other person or style. Let the true you emerge. God desires that we pray to Him in spirit and in truth. The only way we will be able to do that is by receiving His spirit and humbling ourselves before Him. The Bible is written as this: *"Every branch in me that beareth not fruit he taketh away: and every branch that beareth fruit, he purgeth it, that it may bring forth more fruit"* (John 15:2). Once more, we will all bear fruit; but will it be ripe or rotten?

If we, as His chosen generation, would decide to spend more time praying about our troubles rather than complaining about our troubles, then God can intervene in the midst of this trouble. Our minds won't be cluttered and concerned about the trouble. I am reminded of the Scripture in Job 14, *a man born of a woman is a few days and full of trouble.* Therefore, don't worry, just pray because God's got it under control. The relationship to convey secrets, get help and deliverance from secret sins (God knows them all anyway) should be much like the relationship with a spouse, to disclose who you are in honesty and truth without feeling ashamed. God is that outlet for the truth. As you know, God equates a natural marriage to a spiritual marriage throughout the Bible. When you pray, it makes you steadfast (sturdy) in your commitment to the Father and His love for you. We all must keep praying that the Father would be visible in us.

As I think about this great plan the Father had in mind to keep us, He knew that the lines of communication must be open. The ripping of the veil after the death of Jesus, afforded us this opportunity. Therefore, we can come to the altar to petition God for our forgiveness. In reading the Scriptures, we find Jesus going off to pray (communicate) to His Father. Matthew 26:38, 39 says, *"Then he said unto them, my soul is exceeding sorrowful, even unto death: tarry ye here, and watch with me...O my Father, if it be possible, let this cup pass from me: nevertheless, not as I will, but as thou wilt."* It is found here that even Jesus Himself, being Lord of Lords, 100% divine and 100% human, needed to go away several times and communicate with His Father. Jesus was found praying in the Garden of Gethsemane, as great drops of sweat fell from His head as blood. If Jesus needed to pray, submitting to the communication with His Father, we definitely need to pray and fast. He was our example in the Earth.

David Beckham is known as a soccer warrior; Serena and Venus Williams are tennis warriors. As soldiers of this world, they train every day to strengthen their posterity to win, to conquer. So must the children of God; we are people of war. We are spiritual warriors when it comes to the lifestyle found in Christ. We must practice having a prayer life until it becomes natural. As they are warriors in their craft, we should be warriors in ours. Our craft is not of this world; once again, we are spiritual warriors. We pull down strongholds in the realm of the atmosphere, in the heavenly places. As they are victorious in their world, we are victorious in ours. We are conquerors. As some of us cannot dominate their field, neither can they dominate ours. As we practice daily, a movement in the atmosphere will take place and the energy from that will cause a spiritual pushing and momentum to pray more confidently and boldly in the spirit. Satan will also know your name and be afraid, just as he knew Jesus and the disciples' names and was afraid of them. Why? Because when they prayed, the heavens moved and granted excess to them (Acts 19).This prayer momentum shall cause you to activate the gift of tongues and before you know it, you would have prayed 15, 30 minutes, or even an hour. So pray… pray… pray.

Question: How many seconds have you given Him today? How about 10, 30, or even 60 seconds? We give so much time to nonsense.

In this section of this chapter, I have written what prayer does and provided reference Scriptures for your reading.

Prayer:

1. Prayer will change you and not always the situation (Psalm 5).

2. Prayer gives you wisdom, peace and spiritual insight.

3. Prayer changes your perspective of what you think about yourself.

4. Prayer encourages you and changes your outlook on life and people.

5. Prayer trains your spirit and ear to hear the voice of God.

6. Prayer makes you a spiritual marksman (Psalm 140).

7. Prayer makes us deny ourselves and thirst more for God (Psalm 42:1).

8. Prayer will qualify you, not deny you (Psalm 61).

9. Prayer sets the captive free (Psalm 62).

10. Prayer catapults you from the earthly realm to the spiritual (Psalm 95).

11. Prayer leads and guides you into all truth and understanding (Psalm 27).

12. Prayer makes us love those that some say are unlovable.

13. Prayer makes us love our neighbor and treat everybody right (Psalm 34).

14. Prayer makes us hate sin and love righteousness (Psalm 86).

15. Prayer makes us see beyond the natural things.

16. Prayer helps us prepare for things in the natural/spirit.

Below are examples of prayers, as well as some instructions. Are you ready for warfare? I would say you are. If you follow these instructions, you too shall have a *bulletproof* prayer life. On your mark, get set, pray!

Take authority and command the enemy to go the dry place. Remember, the kingdom of God suffers violence and the violent take it by force.

"Father, your word says that one can put a thousand demons to flight. I take authority in the name of Jesus over everything that comes against the knowledge of God. I pull down every strong hold, casting down imaginations, and every high thing that exalts itself against the knowledge of God, and bring into captivity, every thought to the obedience of God."

"Father, in the name of Jesus, I take back everything the devil stole. I take back my peace, joy, hope, faith, children, home, and freedom. I shall not be bound. I bind your hands, Satan, on these things in Jesus' name. I loose every gift and all peace, joy, hope, and faith over my children and my home."

The Word of God tells me to prosper and be in good health, even as my soul prospers in Jesus' name. Whenever you bind (stop) something in the earth, it is then bound (stopped) in the heavens. In Matthew 16:19, it says that *whatever you bind on earth shall be bound in heaven and whatever you loose on earth shall be loosed in heaven.*

You have power to decree a thing in prayer.

You cannot just start binding and there is no loosing, and vice versa. That's against spiritual laws. You must rebuke the curse and then release the blessings in the earth in Jesus' name. Let's continue on. We must arrest the language in prayer of telling the devil to go back to hell from where he came. The devil laughs at the sound of that because he did not come from there; that only happens at the end. He was the creation of God. He was the chief praise and worship leader, who was thrown from heaven unto the earth. His time of total defeat has not come yet. Therefore, he didn't come from hell.

Command him to go to the dry places in the atmosphere, where he cannot use the same trickery that same way he once used them. When you bind, you must loose; when you decree, you must declare. You must violently take back your mental stability, healings, deliverances, marriage, finances, power and render the devil powerless in your life in Jesus' name. Remind him that you execute authority, this day, over him. Remind him that the fiery darts, plans, bulls-eye, traps and snares that he assigned to you and your family won't work. Cut him off at the point of entry and decree and declare a thing. Are you covering your household before going to work, school, shopping, or just in your leisure at home? The devil never takes a break, so why should we? Salvation is a seven- days-a-week job. If you intend to stay employed by God, you must be vicious about keeping what belongs to you out of the hands of the enemy. Yes, that's what he is, your enemy. Keep him at bay with prayer and fasting. This will bruise him effectively. He wants to steal, kill and destroy you including everything you're connected to.

Beloved, please do not forget to pray for your pastor(s) and their families; we need it. As pastors, we come under attack often and it's not always from outside of the church. Saints, please hear me and hear me good. Sometimes, it is a struggle for us daily and you don't know the hell we have gone through just to get to Sunday morning service or weekday Bible class. This is not an easy calling to be in. It may seem glamorous; however, this is a ministry of labor and love. So, cover us in your prayers and shower us with your love and understanding as we do the same. Press on to seek the Father in prayer and fasting, and watch God move on your and behalf. *The effective, fervent prayer of a righteous man avails much* (James 5:16). *Pray without ceasing; in everything give thanks, for this is the will of God in Christ Jesus* (1Thessalonians 5:17-18). Go on and fight, prayer warrior; that you may be able to stand in the evil day. Whenever, wherever you pray, please don't forget to pray in Jesus' name, even more, *After the Alter*. Amen.

5

CHURCH FLOW

In the world we live in today, it is amazing to me what we, as the 21st century church, has deemed "church flow" to be. I know it's something we do and say concerning the fabric we wear on our backs; the display of flashy watches and expensive shoes we carefully put on our pedicured feet on any given Sunday. Still, it leaves something to be desired. This mania has run rapid in the church and gone viral on all social media. Even amongst those who do not frequent the church, they too, are familiar with the "church flow" attire. Nonetheless, I would like to convey to you the heart of God concerning this thing called "church flow."

The Father desires that we look at this with a *spiritual eye* and not a natural eye. I don't know who, where or when this thing started, but I was sent to see and then say at this point that there is something much more unnerving and spiritual behind this movement. He, the

Father says, *"The life is more than meat, and the body is more than raiment"*. (Luke 12: 23). This is not at all holy, but a means to a dreadful end. I am not trying to be deep; just being obedient. I beseech thee, please don't stop reading now. Although you may think it's alright, the Father has set it in my spirit to write about what's on His mind and how this relates to salvation and our *After the Alter* experience.

Sunday morning church flow in the eyes of God has been dummied down to meet and greets. A fashion show of sorts, few scriptures read, and an array of songs being sang by some whose hearts are far from Him. He says that our worship encounters with Him has become lucent and lukewarm at best, meaning you're neither hot nor cold in your desire for Him. He wishes we would be one or the other. He continued on to say that the selection of songs rendered have great meanings, but come from forgotten souls. He says for some, the music may ring well on the outside for others; yet, to Him the Father, it clatters ugly on the inside. Some of you will catch that later. He feels that we, as the church, are more concerned with the treasures here on earth, rather than the treasures that are laid up in heaven. Have we been so focused on our Sunday morning apparel that we have become less concerned about the souls lost on the very same Sunday morning? Do we, as the church, not recognize that this "church flow" facade is another diversion and a divisive scheme of the enemy?. God continued on to say, because men have become lovers of themselves, the church has become more about their outer appearance rather than their inner appearance. This has brought about another schism for the world to lose respect for the church at large. He says, "The world has gotten their training from the church and has made church more about them, than *me,*" says the Lord of Host! The Bible speaks of Christians to not be ignorant of Satan's devices. If we are doing what the world is doing, are they following us, or are we following them? The Father spoke softly in my ears and said, "That some of us are like *whited sepulchers, adorned-beautiful to see*, as a bride on her wedding day, *but yet we are full of dead man's bones,* (Matthew 23:27-28), the walking dead. It's more than just a television show. That is not the Father's plan and desire for our lives; but we and this epidemic smells kind of stinky in His nostrils. Now, the Father is not against prosperity, or fine linen. However, He is against whatever distracts us from preaching the good news of Jesus Christ.

Just as the cameras on our cell phones are capturing the brands of styles we wear each Sunday, God is capturing everything that we say and do and it needs to line up with God's logos, (His thoughts).The Father is raising up pastors, teachers, evangelists and prophets, and those alike, who are not afraid to speak out against what displeases Him according to his Word. We are crying out to you, telling you that you cannot see Jesus in peace without salvation in Him. There is a spirit of deception that has swept the land and it has started, dare I say it…in the pulpit. Many have withdrawn from attending church due to feelings as if they do not possess the correct attire to attend our churches. Some of this falsehood has come from the sacred place: the pulpit. Pastors, we must change the misconception that a person must be "dressed to the nines" before attending a service. Pastors, some of us spend more time on our church attire than studying the message to bring to church. We are fading away to this age.

Now the Bible plainly says seek the kingdom of God and its righteousness, and all things will be added to you (Matthew 6:33). When seeking the kingdom, God is admonishing that we seek His way of doing things. He is instructing us to live the set-apart life He has designed for us; *"To be not conformed to this word, but be ye transformed by the renewing of your mind"* (Romans 12:2a). We should be on a quest for His presence and the movement of the kingdom of God. Without the kingdom flowing on the inside, we are nothing. Without the kingdom moving within the service each Sunday, Saturday or whenever you meet, we are just a sounding brass and a tinkling cymbal. The right church flow brings revelation, sanctification, and then restoration. Without the flow of anointing in our lives, our church flow is meaningless and an occupied, two-hour ritual ceremony at best. When there is no presence of God, there is no power, no repentance nor deliverance. Saints, the more we pour out before Him, the more He pours Himself into us. God will not dwell where He is not invited nor wanted because of our own agendas. We have gotten lost in the wrong church flow of life.

As mentioned earlier in this book, what does it profit a person to have a form of godliness and deny the power thereof? We end up having a service overflowing with pomp and circumstance. He's coming back for a church, His church- His bride, without a spot, wrinkles or blemish. Not what *we,* have made the church. We worry too much about the outer appearance and nothing about the dead man's bones the souls are carrying around daily. *Saints, refocus!*

The church flow should be people asking the Spirit of God to flow-flow in me and around this place. The Lord declares He is searching for a people that will worship Him in spirit and in truth. We need a renewed mind. Holiness is taking off the old man and putting on the new man. That is the removal of carnality we once walked in, and allowing God to change our superficial mindset to please Him. The correct church flow does this. The spirit of God moves freely in a welcomed atmosphere. The spirit of God will begin to change how we look at ourselves in reference to our holy appearance. I am truly shaking my head, but more importantly, God, is shaking His head at our foolery and ignorance to what's truly at stake here-the soul of a man. I am reminded of the Scripture in Mark 7, which speaks of *what defiles a man*. I read nothing that speaks of the raiment, the attire of a man. But, Jesus speaks on the wickedness that flows from a man's heart that keeps him out of the will, i.e., that defiles a man and deems him separated from the Father.

On Sunday morning, there will be many who will enter our churches for many reasons. As laymen in the God's vineyard, we know everyone is not coming to have an experience or encounter with Jesus at these services. Many will come, and do come out of tradition. Many will come for literally the fishes and the loaves. Many will come because they heard about the praise team. Many will come to hear what the preacher has to say about helping the needy. Many will come to see the preacher in person because they got hooked on their personality from social media. Others will even come to get a glance at the first lady or to see if there is one. Don't get it twisted; there are some strange people in the world. There will be a few who are Sunday morning church junkies as drug abusers, getting a fix for the week. However, remaining the same; by choice. They are bound and need to be set free. Alas, a few will come to be saved and to learn how to live holy, truly; if it's preached. *Holiness* seems to be a curse word nowadays.

God is calling out the masked preachers to preach the real Gospel of Jesus Christ. The cross! Regardless of who may oppose this Gospel and may be preaching some other kind. Assuredly, John the Baptist did not have a fashion consultant. Truly, the earth groans and moans for the true men and women of God to trend the streets, bridges and the places that the loveless go to escape everyday life. It's time for us to get out of our cushy pulpits and reach out beyond the walls. I am reminded of Matthew 9, which paraphrased is this: Jesus tells the Pharisees, *I was not sent to those who do not need a Physician, but to those who do* (found also in Mark 2:17). If we desire the miracles of the Bible, then we need to do as Jesus and the Apostles did in the Bible. If we are not doing as they did, by preaching and teaching salvation and holiness, everything else is superficial, including the songs we sing and the prayers we pray. None of this means a thing. God counts it all dung.

To the saints who are unsure of the apparel to wear on Sundays (as some of you are caught up in the "Sunday morning church flow" of social media): wear what you have, pray over yourselves and allow God to lead you. Believe me this day; if you submit your hearts to the cause of Christ, He will lead, direct, and bless you with some flow attire of your own. Don't allow anyone to set you up for failure and keep you from the altar because of the fabric you wear. Set your feet pointed towards the church house the next time the doors are open.

If you are a pastor reading this book, I have questions. What does your Sunday morning church flow look like? Are you in intense worship with an expectation of God's presence? Are you allowing God to flow regardless of how you studied the night before? Is it about you and what you are wearing? Are you so traditionalized that you miss the move of God? What exactly does your church flow look like? Are you more concentrated on the membership or visitation, counting the flow of tithes and offerings?

Yes, those things have its place; but, this

can't be more important than what the Jesus died for. Picture what God is saying about what Sunday morning church flow should express to Him. Go with me into the mind of God pertaining to this. God's church flow appears as this. God enters into His gates with thanksgiving and entering into his courts with praise. His children are praising Him in the dance and with the psaltery and harp. His children are praising Him with the strings and organs. His children are praising Him with the sound of the trumpet. His children are crying out as the angels do, singing 'holy, holy, holy' around His throne (at His altar).

His children are worshipping Him with their whole hearts and in reverence of holiness. His ministers are preaching the Gospel with fire and anointing. When God's glory fills the room, He hovers by His spirit and then sits on the people, as His praises goes forth. When my spirit is in the building, God is saying, the lame walk, the blinded eyes open, the sick are healed from all infirmities and the unsaved is saved and set free. This is what God's Sunday morning church flow looks like to Him.

Just picture it in your minds: the Body of Christ worshipping Him in spirit and in truth, with a harmonious sound that cannot be ignored. The glory is flowing so thick in your sanctuary, the angels come and sit alongside your walls, as the King of glory comes in. Everyone is kneeling and bowing down in worship as you spiritually see the blood streaming down from the throne of grace where you stand, (those who have an ear to hear and eyes to see). Salvation Himself has entered the room. This is what church flow looks like. I admonish you to wake up out of your sleep and put away this unwise decision to follow the crowd that says what church flow is and what some of us, too, has adopted it to be.

We, as pastors, are to guide the sheep, not do what they do. We are to guide them, not derail them. We will be held accountable for such idiocy. Saints, stop getting caught up in this mess as well; we need to major in what's important to God and not be diverted by the devil's plots and plans to steer us away from God's heart. For life is more than raiment; for all of that shall pass away! But what we wear on the inside is what glorifies God, and that, my friend, is what *Sunday morning church flow is made of!* You can get it, *After the Alter*. Amen.

6

FORGIVING PAST THE PAIN

They berated our Lord throughout the streets outside of Jerusalem; men, women, and children spat on him and taunted Him as the soldiers continued to beat him. They hauled Him from judgment hall to judgment hall as they made Him a spectacle for all to gaze upon. The Bible makes clear that Jesus did not say a word. The Bible explains that the people teased Him, the soldiers slapped Him on every side and mocked Him saying, *"Prophesy unto us, thou Christ, Who is he that smote thee?"* (Matthew 26:68). They laughed and ridiculed our Lord, the Savior of the world. The soldiers "encouraged Him" with whips and chains to carry His coffin cross on His back, as some watched in horror as He slowly walked to His fate on the dirt road to Golgotha. He was so badly beaten He could barely stand. Yet, through all of this, His sufferings, He continued to go and walk to a place of death, Golgotha, which was nicknamed the place of the skull.

Calvary! Why, because His love for us is intentional and unconditional. *"What is man that he is mindful of him?"* (Psalm 8:4a) I can imagine in my mind that they probably kicked him a few times, even though the Bible does not allude to this. Can you imagine how many participators with names never mentioned in the Bible threw stones at Him? He was...a dead man walking. Can you see Jesus? Can you see Jesus shaking His head in pain; I picture Him with tears rolling down His face. The Bible doesn't really clarify that, however, the Bible does suggest that He understands everything we have gone through, will go through, and is going through at the point of you examining this book. This includes the pains and strains when pulling the knife out of our very own back, stabbed by those who alleged that they loved us. I want to include the accusations, the lies, and the social injustices that were meant to assassinate our character. But, the Bible declares that *"No weapon that is formed against thee shall prosper"* (Isaiah 54:17a), if you are the dead in Christ.

Jesus has already been there, and as we

read the Gospels, Jesus' situation is playing out right before our very own eyes. Through His bruised and bleeding eyes, He could see the same ones He healed from all types of diseases and infirmities just standing by, too afraid to aid Him. I imagine some of them were whispering to Him, "Jesus, save yourself." After fixing their eyes on Him, they turned their backs on Him. No doubt He was feeling rejected; but yet, He loved us. I am sure He was feeling hurt and disappointed after all He had done. Certainly, all the Pharisees and Sadducees were there observing, course jesting. Presuming He was getting a "King of the Jews'" reward; the crucifixion. Just what He deserved!

Can you see it as I explain it to you? As He walked, sometimes falling down to His knees, not only because of the pain, but, because He needed to show us that life will get heavy oftentimes. However, we can get back up as He did as He carried that old rugged cross. He fell down on His knees to show us where we should be when life overwhelms us; on our knees, in earnest prayer. I believe He fell down to show us the ultimate humility, knowing who and whose He is. He could have called on a legion of warring angels to fight for Him. But, He stayed the course to Calvary. Jesus was being persecuted by the very ones on whose behalf He worked miracles for. He, every now and then assuredly had to crawl with the weight of that cross on His shoulders; signifying the weight of the world. I am reminded that in Isaiah 53:5 that *"He was wounded for our transgressions, He was bruised for our iniquities: the chastisement of our peace was upon him..."* I fashioned in my mind that there must have been some blood on that tree. The blood, His blood dripping from His head as He wiped it away from His brow with his hand as He carried that cross.

Allow me to paint the picture for you. Envision our Savior shifting the cross from side to side as He stumbled down the dirt road to Golgotha, hardly able to keep His balance. Why did He do it? Because He saw us afar off...and endured the agony? When He finally got to the destination, the place where they were to hang our King, our Lord and Savior Jesus Christ, the anointed one, no doubt the soldiers continued to scuff at Him as they hung Him high and stretched Him wide. Jesus, for us, the Savior died.

Listen, child of God, as I pause to gather myself and give you a moment to reflect. God is sympathetic right here and wants you to understand that He knows they betrayed you; but, love them anyhow. He was our model to show that we can. I know they deeply hurt you; again, love them. He says He hasn't forgotten His pain, but you and I were worth it. Even if that the man or woman took your child away through violence, continue to live and forgive. I am saying, the Father recognizes our valleys; but, you can get through it and you will go through it!

Jesus. As Jesus hung on that cross from the sixth to the ninth hour, the blood streamed down for you and me. The excruciating pain hit Him on every side, not just the pain from the punches or the way they bullied Him. Not even the pain because they pierced Him in His side (imagine surgery without anesthesia) and watched the blood and water gush out like a busted pipe. It was the pain of us crucifying Him over and over again through our sins; our reckless lives. After all of this, He still loved us...He did not come down off that cross. Oh, what love! Even though we weren't there, we were all guilty!

Please understand, just as Jesus continued to love them, He also forgave them. Jesus is saying not only must you love those who hurt you, but you must also forgive those who hurt you. Although Jesus was greatly hurting spiritually and physically, Jesus mustered up enough strength to whisper to the Father, this amazing request. Pay close attention to this. In Luke 23:34, He looked up to His Father and He said, *"Father, forgive them, for they know not what they do."* That's forgiveness!

Once again, God is saying, I know he beat you, but, you must love him enough to forgive him. He is not saying, *stay*. He is saying *forgive* him. I know you got a little "baby daddy drama," let him go. God is saying, "I am here, daughter; truly, I am your source…lean on me." God is saying to you, "I know somebody took your innocence away at a young age against your will; whether you are male or female, I too suffered the same." But, if you forgive them, you'll be the better for it. You'll be able to do this through Christ who strengthens you, and be able to look them right in their faces and not feel the pain anymore.

Sir, I know she hurt you and won't let you see your children; forgive her, and take it to Jesus. He can turn that heart of stone into a heart of flesh and turn it around in your favor. Woman, I know he left you to raise those babies on your own. You must forgive him, too, and love and see him through Christ. I understand that they broke your heart, my sister, my brother, into many pieces. Nevertheless, God can restore and give you better than what you had…forgive them.

You can't afford to carry hatred and claim the name of Jesus Christ. God is asking, *"For he that loveth not his brother whom he hath seen, how can he love God whom he hath not seen?"* (1 John 4:20). The Father says you are a liar. Basically, God is saying the love of the Father is not in you and me. I know it's a difficult thing for the Father to ask-to love someone, to forgive someone who despitefully used you; who hurt you. He too, has been hurt and is consistently hurt by the choices we make. The Father does not force His love or His will for our lives; *After the Alter*. However, He desires that we hear His voice and obey willingly.

Therefore, we must *pray for those that hurt us* (Luke 6:28). God is saying *"For if ye forgive men their trespasses, your heavenly Father will also forgive you"* (Matthew 6:14). This prayer Jesus even taught to His disciples. There is peace in forgiveness. Now catch this: He asked the Father to not only forgive them for what they do, but He was asking the Father to forgive "us" for all the stuff He saw us do afar off. He was asking God to forgive us, for our future mess. Did you get that? He was asking God to forgive us for the wrongs that we do, and will do; our past, current and even future sins. The Bible expresses that we crucify Him afresh each and every time we sin against Him.

I want to get this statement stuck in your head, so you may be mindful when you are being tempted and drawn away by your desires planted by the devil. He forgave us then, how can we not forgive them now? You need to know that you must forgive, so that you can live. The Bible explains that as He hung on the cross, that there was darkness throughout the earth. Listen, you may feel as Jesus did, left in a dark place. But I tell you that if you forgive, the darkness will be no more and the light shall appear once again in your life, after you leave it all at the altar. You may feel abandoned, forsaken and broken. Nonetheless, the Bible answers and declares that *He will never leave you nor forsake you* (Hebrews 13:5). Jesus is always near.

There is a glorious release in forgiveness, because the Father will *give you beauty for those ashes* (Isaiah 61:3). God had to forsake Jesus, to forgive us. Jesus, at those moments, was bearing the sins of the world. Because God could not look upon what Jesus had become (*sin*), God had to forsake part of Himself, just to restore us. Through that restoration, we have become new creatures in God, *new wine vessels* (2 Corinthians 5:17). Surrender all the debris, all the broken branches and pieces of straw attached to your skin (spirit) from the last winemaker (Devil, carnal mind) and allow the Father to pour new wine (Himself) into the new you (your redeemed spirit).

The Lord wants you to know that you can believe, repent, and be healed of un-forgiveness at this very moment. I want you to know that saying that you are saved isn't' enough; you must walk in forgiveness. This thing can cause anxiety, stress and a drawback spirit in your life, creating a dark pit you can't get out of. You cannot walk in God and walk in un-forgiveness; the two are not equal. I am telling you that God is not pleased with that. You must forgive them, through the pain.

Pastors, we are included in this as well. We are not free from this commandment just because we said, "Yes!" We should be the first partakers of forgiveness. We, too, must love and forgive them through the pain. Our Father knows they tried to speak against our integrity and sabotage our dreams; we must love them, in spite of. We are not exempt from guilt and shame; however, thank God it's all under the blood of Jesus. Various things will happen and be said, simply because we bear *His* name. We, who carry the mantle to feed the sheep, are the first partakers of this madness. Stoning, slandering and backbiting were a part of the job when we told the Lord, "Yes, send me Lord, I'll go." Just be sure you're not the one who is carrying a few stones in your pocket when He calls your name.

Therefore, the Father is saying, "Get yourselves together and remember His Son endured the cross." If they hated Him, they will hate you! Brethren, take your emotions out of it and look at the spirit of discord behind it. It is spiritual warfare, baby; so pull yourself up by your bootstraps, and run this race with patience and endurance. Whether they are saints or "a'ints," the devil will use whosoever is willing to yield their bodies to him. Listen, God will repay and set a table before you in the presence of your enemies (Psalm 23). May I remind you that the Word of God is written as this, *"Who shall lay any thing to the charge of God's elect? It is God that justfieth"* (Romans 8:33).

We are to be examples in our public lives as well as our private lives to show the same grace to others as God has shown towards us. Remember when Peter asked Jesus in Matthew 18:21, *concerning how many times shall my brother sin against me and I forgive him, till seven times?* Jesus answered by saying, *"I say not seven times, but seventy times seventy."* This means that our forgiveness towards our brethren should be unlimited if we have the kingdom of God living in us. I realize we are not Jesus; yet, we are commanded to turn the other cheek; not in shame, but in humility. Beloved, as long as we live, in these mortal bodies, we will be faced with naysayers and prognosticators; we shall suffer persecution, including those who wear the collar. Nonetheless, we must continue to love and forgive all.

Don't allow your emotions to divert you from your calling. The Father knows that they have rejected you. That is so He can elevate you. Remember, *"For promotion cometh neither from the east, nor from the west, nor from the south. But, God is the judge: he putteth down one and setteth up another"* (Psalm 75:6-7). God is saying that He shall bring every high place down before you. I know you're bleeding from the pain on every side. Pastors and preachers, *we* must forgive them all; we've been carrying that church hurt too long.

Some of us get into our pulpits every Sunday preaching out of an abused and unforgiving spirit. We must be in peace and be holy, *for without it, no man will see God,* (Hebrews 12:14). I know you feel as if sometimes they hung you on a tree, but Gods' Word says to show them the same grace that we've have been shown. I am admonishing you not to allow nothing or nobody to separate you from the love of God in

Christ Jesus. Forgive them and move on. *It is finished!* You must be free... so your sheep can be free. You must be delivered to teach boldly on deliverance. It's a sad commentary to think that many of us are preaching in this area and yet we are not free. *Let it go.* You must be free; to live in this freedom, which Jesus' blood bought for you. Your life literally depends on it. Each day God gives you breath to breathe, you must take the time to forgive those who have trespassed against you. To walk in godliness, you must walk in wholeness and that can't come without total surrender to God, to His purpose and plan. Can I tell you that most times, those things that happened in your life were just a set up? They were allowed for the purpose. You see, those things didn't kill you; therefore, God now will use it to build you. Brethren, you were not built to break. The Bible says that *"They intended evil against thee: they imagined a mischievous device, which they are not able to perform"* (Psalm 21:11). In other words, we know what the devil meant for evil, God will turn it around for our good. Stop holding on to folks. Some of those folks are dead and gone, and you're still holding on to your past.

Listen, that's what it is; *your past*. As you should know, the Bible says that *He that the son (Jesus) set free, is free indeed* (John 8:36). He made us free the moment He shed His blood and said, "It is finished" and gave up the ghost.

In closing, only God can close those wounds and heal the pain you have inside. Healing can start when you love them and forgive them past the pain. You have a destiny to fulfill and the devil, your adversary, is trying to destroy you by constantly hanging those drapes of reminders in your mind. *Let it go*. You may still have some bruises, but baby, trust and know; you are healed. Receive this and take it to the altar!

I recognize that forgiveness is a touchy subject, but it's one that needs to be explored. I realize un-forgiveness has saturated the hearts and very core of many within the body of Christ. In spite of this, we have the audacity to walk in pride and have a sanctimonious arrogance about ourselves. Believe me, God's eyes see all. We must ask God to heal us from past and present hurts. As believers, we cannot allow this to reign in our mortal bodies. In order to live a successful life in Christ, we ought to be steadfast in forgiveness.

I know it hurts and feels better to hold on to death, because the truth is that un-forgiveness is death. Satan would love to have you, and as long as you remain in the state of un-forgiveness, you are in known sin. Kick the devil off your left shoulder and commit to forgiving. Yes, it is written in the Bible that the spirit is willing, but the flesh is weak. Nevertheless, through prayer, all things are possible with God. Don't let un-forgiveness send you to the lake of fire. Because there is one thing that is true; misery really does love company and if there is someone or something in your life keeping you in that place, that place of depression, oppression, and un-forgiveness…run.

Everything that Jesus went through before and during the cross, He yet loved us, forgave us, and unselfishly died for us. He never considered Himself. Jesus was the ultimate example of forgiveness and love. Brethren, forgive now while you still have that red hot lava running through your veins. Forgive now while your heart continues to beat. Don't let un-forgiveness separate you from the King and His kingdom. Humble yourselves, put away strife and self-will so that he that stole from you will steal no more. Count it as robbery, because you have no peace in this area. Do not allow the devil to continue to rob you of your inheritance into eternal life of joy with Jesus Christ. The old saints used to say, "Don't let it be said too late." With forgiveness in mind, forgive those who have trespassed against you, whether they are alive or gone. Come, let us go to the altar and pray:

Heavenly Father, I thank You that You hear me when I pray. I praise You Father, for You are great, holy and the God who forgives all sin. I am sure You can take it from there.

Remember, forgiveness starts with you, *After the Alter*. Amen.

7

CHANGING ALTARS

Marriage is an inheritance and not to be entered into lightly. The new couple moves from the single life into the life of accountability to one another. However, they are not only accountable to themselves, but unto the God for which they entered into this sacred union; it is a three-fold cord created by God. God tells us in his word that a man (he) that finds a wife, meaning his heart has desired a wife; therefore, he searches for her until he finds her. Once he feels he has found "the one", his heart turns only to her and the planning can begin. The Bible goes on to say that in looking/searching for what has completed him (Genesis 2:23-25), he *"findeth a good thing and obtaineth favor of the Lord"* (Proverbs 18:22). A man obtains favor and a women obtains a covering, her protector. Proverbs tells us that T*the heart of her husband doth safely trust in her, so that he shall have no need of spoil"* (Proverbs 31:11). This is in accordance to her being the Proverbs 31 wife. It is very important to understand that Proverbs calls her a "wife", not a woman; this has been mistakenly taught over hundreds of years. There is a difference between a woman and a wife in this context; being female does not make you a virtuous woman and certainly not a wife.

Spiritual marriage is also an inheritance and not to be entered into lightly. At the point of decision, your life or your body are no longer your own. As a submitted vessel unto God, you are a bondservant unto the Father (Romans 1:1). When entering into this type of marriage, we go from being a spiritual peasant to royalty...a royal priesthood, a chosen generation (I Peter 2:9). In our decision to vacate, we move from a spiritual pit to a spiritual palace. We have an inheritance with God by the blood through the death, burial, and resurrection of Jesus Christ. Guess what? The only way out is death! We have all the same rights and privileges as Jesus because we are a part of a new family looing onward to a new home. We are no longer looking inside from the outside, but we are looking outside from the inside, from the safety of the same aforementioned palace. Simply, we have exchanged our altar of death for an altar of life in Jesus Christ where we will always be subject to a lifetime of alterations at the altar.

Oftentimes, before the wedding takes place, a bride will need to lose weight, which she does by following a strict diet. The Bible says *to lay aside every weight and the sin* (as the glory comes with weight, sin has a heaviness also – the lust of the eyes, flesh, and pride of life) *that so easily besets us,* the thing or things that separate us from Christ and *"let us run with patience the race that is before us"* (Hebrews 12:1b). The race before the bride and us is becoming one with the groom. We lay aside the weight of sin when we adhere to strict principles given in God's word. Because as the brides' dress sometimes will need much altering after the weight loss so that dress fits perfectly on her special day, we also need constant altering on the Potter's wheel to fit perfectly into our eternal garments. The Father is the greatest seamstress ever! The Bible was written for those who have decide to come unto Him as a battered lover to be healed into a blushing bride; therefore, we need altering.

Don't be fooled by the once saved, always

saved cliché...it's not true. Those who live from this principle have been bamboozled and will spend eternity after the judgment in hell. Many believe this across America in many denominations and its simply false doctrine. You cannot walk away from the altar of God to practice a lifestyle of sin and expect God to say, *"well done"* and go free. He is a God that judges (I Corinthians 6:3-5 and 2 Peter 2: 4-10). A spiritual alteration for His name is a cutting away of excess baggage and demonic forces so that we can retain our bridal glow. A bride's dress will always suffer a little altering, whether it's new or old; if the dress is going to fit, it must be snipped! In God, the process of altering is painful, but necessary if we are going to have the spiritual wedding of our dreams. We want to ask the Father for what we want, but He says to *"present your bodies a living sacrifice"* (Romans 12:1). We must be willing to sacrifice and change altars to receive the kingdom to its fullness.

The book of Ruth is a great example of changing altars. Ruth was a woman who was from the land of the Moabites. As the story goes, Ruth is met by a family from Bethlehem-

Judah who came to the land of Moab because famine arose in their homeland. Escaping for their lives, the family consisted of a father, mother, and two sons who all practiced the religion of Judaism. Ruth practiced and worshipped the pagan god Chemosh. The worshipping of this pagan god and other gods, plus the death of her husband caused Ruth to make an executive decision during one of the most difficult times in a young child-bearing women's life. After all, Naomi, her mother-in-law, and her family left a place of praise to go to a place of death and pagan gods in the land of Lot's grandsons, the Moabites. I can imagine in my mind that Ruth saw in Naomi the strength from her God that she had never experienced from a pagan god. Naomi's God made a great impression on Ruth simply by the way she lived and worshipped. You can tell by the way she made the declaration. *I am not leaving you. I will denounce my god and I will serve* (marry) *your God and He will become my God.* At that very moment was a changing of altars in Ruth's life. Ruth gave her god its divorce papers and sought after Naomi to learn more about Jehovah-Jireh (provider).

Ruth was accustomed to superstitious rituals and graven images. She was the granddaughter of Eglon, king of Moab, who was the grandson of Balak, the king of Moab during Moses' time. It is recorded that both of these kings had a less than friendly relationship with the Israelites (as recorded in Numbers 22-24). Ruth, although a Moabite princess, she denounced her life as a pagan princess for the life of a kingdom princess because she went to Judaism, and later into Christianity. Ruth was focused on the book that was right in front of her…Naomi. She proceeded to say "Yes" to the dress. As you continue to study the text, it was almost as if she was saying "I don't know what's going to come, but I am not staying here to die". She did not look back as Lot's wife; she followed Christ in following Naomi. She sought alterations at a different altar. I believe she realized the other altar was empty and had no life desired. Basically, she told Naomi in so many words, "I must let go; let's go." Ruth inherited greatness because she released the accursed thing so that she could unknowingly be blessed. There's no doubt in my mind that Ruth watched Naomi serve her God and saw results. She desired that same type of relationship or kind of worship.

Understand those who live or confess to live in Christ are a much watched book. You will become a watched epistle for many a far off and up close. Many will watch how you worship at the actual altar and at the altar of life to see if you are really "sold out" for Christ. Ruth did not know how her future would turn out, but she was very familiar with her past. I sensed that she was more drawn to what was in front of her than behind her; it was as if she was in the famine of her life. We are sometimes faced with a void that leads to feelings of emptiness and despair. That empty place is the lack of Jesus in our lives. Ruth did not look back as Lot's wife; she followed Christ in following Naomi. God beckoned Ruth in a roundabout way to change through Naomi. God is also calling you to a higher place in Him. Just in case you don't know how the story ends, I'll provide a synopsis. Ruth meets Boaz, some wealthy kindred, married him and is restored a hundredfold. Ruth was restored and recompensed for being a faithful daughter even after the death of her husband. Ruth went from gleaning in the field to owning the fields. Boaz received favor and his good thing; Ruth received her protector, covering, and wealth, because she obeyed the voice of her mother-in-law. Ruth did not lean to her own thoughts and ideologies but towards the wisdom of God in Naomi (Proverbs 3:5-6). Ruth traded a lesser for a better and became the lineage to Jesus Christ since she and Boaz were the great-grandparents to King David. Talk about restoration! God had a plan for her and He has a plan to restore us back to our rightful inheritance, if we obey.

This story admonishes a new thought process and submission to God's plans and ideas for our lives, i.e. changing our altars for His altar and alterations. As a natural husband enjoys introducing and presenting his bride to others, God desires to do the same with you and I to the world, and to the heavenly host. The Bible tells us that the angels rejoice over one soul that comes home; God is married to the backslide and the new convert. It is time to come home permanently and receive your priestly attire. The Father is rolling out the red carpet and calling many to come to the wedding at the royal palace to dine at the royal table with kings and queens. Come one, come all. Take off your grave clothes and get your inheritance, *After the Alter*. Amen.

8

MIND GAMES

"For to be carnally minded is death; but to be spiritually minded is life and peace. Because the carnal mind is enmity against GOD: for it is not subject to the law of God, neither indeed can be (Romans 8:6-7).

I once read somewhere that the brain or cerebral cortex, as it is medically known, is a great mystery. It's such a mystery, that scientists and neurobiologists have spent many years and billions of dollars trying to comprehend the exact structure of its function. Trying to fathom how the conscious mind and the subconscious mind seems to be one. However, it functions as a separate entity of its own, meaning it does two different things although it's stored in the same place... the brain. Many can search the world all over (they've tried) for the answers, but they will never find, unless they know the Creator. This is a God thing, and He has *wonderfully made us*. As stated in Genesis 1: 26-27, *"Let us make man in our image, after our likeness…in the image of God created he him; male and female created he them"*.

All that being said, how can a scientist know the mind of Christ? They can't, unless they receive God's spirit. So then, scientists can spend an eternity pondering over these things, trying to understand the complexities of the mind, gaining knowledge, but never finding the full truth.

Beloved, as you have read in the previous chapters, because He is spirit and we dwell in the flesh, only way we can grasp these mysteries is by being filled with His spirit by faith. The Bible declares that we will not know or apprehend *all* things until we meet the Book (the writer, creator, the Lord God, Jesus Christ) face to face. "Why must we wait until then?" might be your question, if you are a new saint, that is. It's because our natural mind, thoughts, and physical bodies cannot conceive or handle the totality of the mind of Christ nor the complete essence of which He is; who God really is. I chuckle sometimes with excitement at the thought that we must be naturally dead before we can meet Him, who was once dead … face to face. That's the awesomeness of God.

All of the research and dissertations done in the world cannot explain the omniscience of the all-knowing living God. When I think of the abilities in our bodies and how it works without batteries…God is amazing! He is worthy to be praised. Everything praises Him for being the Creator of it: from the wind to the birds, from the grass that grows and the clouds that give us their presence daily. From every breath we breathe, and every thought we think, He's worthy of our praise. We must praise Him.

I know you're wondering right now, what this has to do with this chapter title. Well, keep reading. You need positive thoughts to achieve success in all areas of your life, but this only comes by shifting the paradigm of your thought pattern. Again, Romans 12:2 says *"Be not be conformed to this world, but be ye transformed by the renewing* (change your thinking) *of your mind, that you may prove* (be an example) *what is that good, and acceptable, and perfect, will of God"*.

Let me help you discover and/or understand the real you, in spirit and in truth, that you may know the truth and this truth will set you free. Example: there was a man who came to Jesus with his son, who was obviously being attacked by a demon of some sort. This demon made him foam at the mouth daily and would try to make the boy commit suicide. The father said to Jesus, *"I brought him to your disciples, but they could not heal him."* After that, Jesus asked the father a very powerful question: *"Do you believe I can do this?"* The man answered with his conscious mind; *"Yes, I believe."* However, the father answered Jesus according to his *carnal mind,* or his flesh, the first time. Jesus always walks in the spirit, because He is 100% spirit/ He is a revealer of all things and He exposed the father's true feelings. As the man stood there, the spirit or light of God immediately convicted the father, and he cried out with a loud voice, the truth. The second time the father said something so powerful. *"Help me with my unbelief"* (Mark 9). In other words, the first answer was false; the second answer was the truth because it was answered by his true identity or subconscious mind, which is where our spirit (our real person) lives. Our real thoughts and feelings lie in the sub-consciousness of our brains, which is where your thoughts are made and exchanged. This is why the Father says that *"a double minded man is unstable in all his ways"* (James 1:8).

Except the Father reveal unto us the identity of having one mindset, we will continue to be obscured when it comes to correct thinking. You see, the father only had mouth faith in the beginning and not heart faith (subconscious faith). God only looks at the heart; man looks at the outward experience. Only the eyes of God know and see the true intent inside our very thoughts. Only God can get our genuine selves to lineup with the Word of God and to be honest about all the hidden, secret places in our hearts. Every belief and unbelief must get in line with the real us. There is nothing the devil can do to us.

People, our real faith lives in our subconscious mind and if we just be honest with ourselves, we can walk in Christ victoriously. You will walk in victory because when you say, "I believe," it will be the honest truth. When you say, "I don't know if I have faith to believe this or that; that will be the truth also." And God can work with that. The truth!

Your deliverance is a state of mind. The

devil does not attack your conscious mind because he knows that the issues of life do not flow from there. He attacks the sub=mind because the real you flows from there (your heart). This is why the Bible says to *"keep thy heart with all diligence; for out of it are the issues of life"* (Proverbs 4:23). We have a dual nature-one of spirit and one that is natural; two mindsets. In order to control your flesh, you must first get control of your nature by bringing it under subjection to the things of God (i.e. self-control). Example: when a man asks his wife questions like, "Where would you like to go for dinner?", "How are you doing today?" or "What name shall we give the baby?", sometimes she will frustrate the man because she has given him several answers to those questions. Usually, by the end of their conversation, the man is usually saying, "Will you please, make up your mind?" She shifts back and forth between both mindsets (opinion of thought) and has not lined them up to say the same thing…*the mind is a battlefield.*

Let me say this right here: Although I have said "women," men can be indecisive as well. We must bring our minds under subjection to the Holy Spirit so we may only think with one, not falling between two opinions. Remember, the enemy is the inner me that wars against daily; it wars against our flesh and our spirit. It is very important that you bring your body and your mind under the authority of Jesus Christ. This can only happen by receiving Him, which houses His spirit and His baptism.

I need you to grasp the tricks of your enemy, the devil. He's after your mind, the authentic you. If you are going to be on the battlefield, you need to know the strategies of your enemy. Believe me, the attack is on and he's moving more rapidly in the earth like never before. He's infiltrating the thoughts, emotions, feelings and desires of God's people, and filling our minds with lies and temptations that cause sin. It all starts with a thought which is planted by the devil. He will lie and wait as a sniper to see if you will fail to pray, and then cause yourself to fall as prey. Then, with one shot (past temptation) it kills you. Understand, because we are three parts (body, soul, and spirit), our flesh rules it all until we make a change, and become born again. Now the Bible lets us know that we are drawn away by our own lust, meaning the desire to sin. We set ourselves up for it. However, the devil does plant the seed. We just listen to how good it sounds and then go after that thing that's burning inside of us to do. I want to remind you again, that the devil's goal is to annihilate you and me spiritually, and then physically. Trust me; he does not bring thoughts that are not attractive or not pleasing to the flesh. It is up to you and me to make a choice about how much and how long we will allow those things to fester and manipulate our flesh. It's a mind game; shake yourself and get out of that stupor before you sin.

Understand that every thought that's not from God is a thought that started from the enemy. Philippians 2:5 says *"Let this mind be in you, which was also in Christ Jesus"*. The word "let" is powerful, because it is a verb; a standing position, allow, release a thing. This text beseeches you to give your mind over to God, to allow Him to dwell freely there so that the Satan will not defeat you. As saints, we slip and slide, perpetuate and perpetrate our true feelings. We hide behind fake smiles and kisses of death (Judas) as if God does not see us.

Don't be fooled; God is not pleased with falsehood of love. If you're struggling with certain sins, then say so. When we confess those things to God, we will be able to receive deliverance from it. Confession is good for the soul. You can hide your heart's mind from the preachers and teachers, but with God, all things are revealed. Remember the seven churches John wrote to? Which one are you? I am not exempt from this scrutiny myself; it takes work and a check in the mirror regularly.

Before I became a pastor, the Father had to chastise me for many years because I thought I could control my life, my thoughts. You see, I was so full of religiosity and traditions of men, I thought I knew more than what I really did. Jesus is not religious, nor is He a Christian. He is God and desires all to be saved and to live the *Bible Out Loud* with a willing heart according to His commandments. I was leaving open many destructive doors from my past and those of my present. Even now as a pastor, I need Him that much more. I need help of the Lord! Let this mind *be*, denotes remaining in a place. The mind of Jesus is incorruptible; a mind that thinks on those things that are pure, what is above and not beneath. I know this is a battle. It stands to reason, that's why God tells us what to think on in Philippians 4:8b *"think on these things"*.

As children, our parents and the older church members always said that an idle mind is the devil's workshop. I found out once I got from under the structure of my mother, that surely they all were correct in that statement. This is still true today. Whether you are five or 50 years old, the devil is still after your mind. If he gets our mind, he knows our thoughts because he will manipulate them whichever way he pleases. He also knows the body will absolutely follow the head attacks. Wherever the head goes mentally, the body will follow. So go back and divorce (renounce) yourself from the covenants you made in the world. You're saved now.

Medical professionals make millions of dollars yearly because of the dent in the prescription drugs due to the darkness that has stolen the minds of many. The devil will torment us with past sins and deeds if we allow him to.

The largest portion of the cortex is called the

association cortex. This lobe is the part that analyzes, processes, and stores information; then, a decision is made. As people of a hurtful or distorted past, we not only process it (the thing), we store it and go back and remember it, as if we forgot that the Bible tells us in Romans 8:1 that *there is no condemnation* (the devil can no longer bring those guilty charges against you to God; you have been released from them) *unto those who walk not according to the flesh, but according to the spirit* (paraphrased). If you didn't know it, you've heard it here. When the enemy tries to remind you of your past; you speak back and say, "Yes I did, but I am saved by grace through faith. I did this and that too, but God delivered me." Remind the devil of the end of the Bible…we win! In other words, at the point of the attack, began to quote scriptures as Jesus did when the devil tempted him and say, *"It is written."*

Surely it does not make sense for you to assemble yourselves with the saints, and leave out the same way you came service after service… bound. Begin to talk back, take back, and curse the devil back. Satan will come after you and your house once you're in the Father's will. You must begin to say what God says about you. It is written in Jeremiah 29:11, *"For I know the thoughts that I think toward you, saith the Lord, thoughts of peace and not of evil to give you an expected end"*. You must get the Word of God and His promises down in your spirit, down in your subconscious, so that your spirit will recall them in the time of storm and attack.

Your walk, your talk, your sanctification, your holiness, and your freedom in Jesus are all up for grabs by the devil. Begin to take it all back. We must safeguard our hearts and minds as soldiers. I know you are saying, "I try not to let my mind wander to ungodliness, but I can't stop myself; I have issues." Slap yourself; the devil, right there, has once again, launched an attack on your mind. You received it, processed it, and then made a bad decision to believe it. Understand that every thought that does not come from God is a thought that started from a lie. Satan has planted it by your emotions and "feelings" of your past, and even some of the present. When he planted it again, you believed it; which makes it the thinker's fault. Although Satan is a lie (fictitious, fabricator, false, deceptive, exaggerator) and the father of those same lies, he cannot be a liar in our lives unless we give him access to our thoughts through open doors and portals. We do this when we neglect *"casting down imaginations and every high thing that exalteth itself against the knowledge* (i.e. understanding) *of God, and bringing into captivity every (the big one) thought to the obedience of Christ"* (2 Corinthians 10:5).

The Bible says he, the devil is a lie…not a liar, and there is a difference. He is unreal in our lives if we practice that level of thinking in our lives. I did not say he didn't exist, I say what the Bible says: "He, the devil, is a lie!" You must come to terms with this to live a victorious life of salvation! If you weren't able to defeat the enemy, Jesus would not have become an example for the entire world to see. You and *I can do all things through Christ who strengthens you,* (Philippians 4:13).

Everyone has a story, even Jesus. Would you like to hear it? Here it goes. After Jesus fasted for forty days and forty nights, the devil tried to tempt Jesus. He spoke three powerful words repetitiously: "It is written." Jesus' mind was already saturated in the Word, so He knew through revelation the plans and devices of His enemy. When there is, again, a relationship with the Father, He will make us privy to those plans as well. It all starts in the mind. The devil took Jesus up in His thoughts, because Jesus was weak from fasting. However, because He was the Word walking; He spoke it! It doesn't matter how long you've been walking this life of salvation, the devil will never give up on coming after you through your mind. Be it one day or 10 years, the enemy won't give up on you and neither will our Father.

I know that in your mind, there is a war that rages; good and bad. Enmity is in us all, it's hidden in our mind (seducing spirits, lying and lustful spirits, etc.). The devil makes it a daily task to attempt, coerce, manipulate and saturate your mind with doubt and fear, and then beat you down as the boxer I mentioned earlier in this book until there is nothing left of you. The devil wants to debase you and then devalue you in the eyes of people, lest you forget the price Jesus paid for you. He really does come to steal, kill and destroy with depression, oppression, suppression, manipulation, ungodliness, low self-esteem, high blood pressure and all kinds of deaths of this world. Howbeit, *Jesus came to give us life and that more abundantly* (John 10:10). Jesus told Peter that *"Satan hath desired to have you, that he may sift you as wheat"*. (Luke 22: 31). Jesus was saying that the devil wants to make you and me defenseless against him, forgetting the power that's within.

There is a slow process of sifting wheat for the purpose of breaking down all the necessary elements, making it bendable for one's usage. Satan's goal is to first play mind games. Then, once you are out of physical and sometimes spiritual strength, he will seek to destroy you. Satan enjoys taking his time attempting to kill us slowly. But aren't you glad that Jesus came that we may have life, and have it more abundantly in Him?

So as you read this chapter, I have one question for you: *Will you please make up your mind?* Will you permit the Father to wash your mind with the blood of Jesus? Remember a carnal mind is enmity with God. So as you are on your journey with Jesus, don't forget to enjoy it. Keep your mind and focus on the internal (kingdom of God) and not the external (it will pass away). *Be in this world, but not of this world* (John 17). Let the mind of Christ overtake you and do not allow your thoughts derail you from your destiny. Say what God says about you. Honestly, it is a game; but it is one you can win. Lean on the Fathers' everlasting arms. Because the inner you, without a makeover, is the enemy...and it's always trying to work against you. If today, when you hear His voice, harden not your heart. Receive His grace, mercy and love. Therefore, gather up the fragments of your mind, plead the blood of Jesus and run this race with confidence in your Heavenly Father.

As noted in the previous chapters, salvation comes at a cost of total surrender and obedience to God. You must deny yourself from control of yourself, for the cross brought you your liberty. Remember; demand your sanity back from the devil, *After the Alter*. Amen.

9

GODHEAD

The Son *"is the expressed image of the invisible God, the firstborn of every creature: For by him were all things created, that are in heaven, and that are in earth, visible and invisible, whether they be thrones, or dominions, or principalities, or powers: all things were created by him, and for him: And he is before all things and by him all things consist. And he is the head of the body, the church: who is the beginning, the firstborn from the dead; that in all things he might have the preeminence. For it pleased the Father that in him should all fullness dwell; and having made peace through the blood of his cross, by him to reconcile all things unto himself; by him, I say, whether they be things in earth, or things in heaven"* (Colossians 1:15-20).

This is a very important chapter that brings all things together and the reasons for the writings you have read thus far, the Godhead. The Word of God in John 1 declares that in the beginning was the word, and the word was God and dwelt amongst us…became flesh. At this moment, I only want to deal with who God is, how He is who He is and how He came to be. Just in case you meet a few unbelievers, you can execute these few findings with them.

Now, I know there may be some who are confused about the Godhead or the deity of Christ. I want to help my brethren who may be in conflict with other religious associations or possibly right there in your own local church. The Godhead refers to the complete manifestation of our Father, who is God in all His attributes and characteristics. He encompasses one person and not three, as some may believe.

Jesus is the humanistic part of this Godhead and was manifested as such, just as the Holy Ghost is a part of this as well. All are the same, entwined in this holy, eternal being, God, our Father. Now, I must tell you the importance of Jesus. Jesus is the center of attention and stands as the point of information in history. All information before Him, speaks about His coming and all history, thereafter. Many believers of the Old Testament and then the New Testament looked for two things during their lives: the coming and the return of our

Lord and Savior, Jesus Christ.

However, those that are looking forward to such a grand event gazed upon and downplayed it as some event that the Paparazzi will be able to capture with film. Woe to these Pharisees; they don't realize that He's coming for the righteous and with judgment in His hand! They will see the God of our salvation; the only living God, the Father, our God who robed Himself in flesh and denied Himself for people who denied Him; this God, we will see. He, who had no sin, became sin to live as a man to be a righteous example.

He, (Jesus) was the one, who paid the ransom for the wretched life of mankind.

Because of this, we owe Him a fee we can never pay. Brethren, I want to share about the nature of Jesus. Our God has perplexed historians for hundreds of years, and yet still boggles the minds of some today. Briefly investigated, Jesus had a dual nature. He was 100% human when He descended on earth, and He is 100% divine. He was God in the flesh. In Luke 1:35, He is referred to as *the holy thing*. The flesh had the *same abilities and desires as any other flesh, yet without sin* (Hebrews 4:15). It is stated in Luke

2:40 that *"the child grew, and waxed strong in spirit, filled with wisdom: and the grace of God was upon Him"*. Jesus got hungry as you and I do. It was flesh. God wanted to show His beloved that we can live a life that is not flawless, but able to withstand.

Jesus commanded His disciples in John 14:26, *to wait for the promise of the Holy Ghost as the Comforter,* because He was leaving them to go back to the Father. This was Jesus showing Himself as a very present help, even though He was ascending back to His father. And so it was in Acts 1:4-5, *"And, being assembled together with them, commanded them that they should not depart from Jerusalem, but wait for the promise of the Father, which, saith he, you have heard of me. For John truly baptized with water; but ye shall be baptized with the Holy Ghost not many days hence"*. The Holy Ghost is God's Spirit manifested in the lives of men in a new relationship. The Holy Ghost is not a separate person from God, but God reveals Himself in another way to man; this is still the same God. As I explain the works of the Holy Ghost, it may seem to some that I am double talking; however, to understand our Father in His beauty, you must have His spirit living in you. Because the Bible says, *a man cannot understand the things of God, unless he has his spirit* [1 Corinthians 2:14 (paraphrased). You and I need His spirit to see things outside of the natural logic of life. I find that this may be the simplest way to explain and describe the almighty God. The way that I convey these things to you has to be done this way.

The Holy Ghost is the third manifestation of God to us. Understanding this is very important once you have received the Father as your Lord and Savior. He is the same spirit that filled the upper room, filled the body and they spoke in other tongues on the day of Pentecost (Acts 1:13). Once you have Him, God dwelling inwardly, He is the very presence of power inside to guide and lead you down the path of righteousness. The term "Holy Ghost" is used *91* times in the New Testament and only four times as the Holy Spirit. Important to note: they are the same. In John 1, where it states *in the beginning was the word and the word was with God and the word was God*, this signifies that the spirit of God was with Him also. So if the Word was with God, and is God, where is this spirit now? It is with us, living in us by His Holy Spirit, and also continues to be with Him, meaning God. No, I am not saying the Spirit of God is no longer where He is. I am saying, He has allowed us to carry a piece of Him everywhere we go because of our relationship with Him so we may walk in the same power Jesus walked in, doing the same things Jesus did while He was here on Earth. It is written in God's Word that greater things shall we do. That only comes by having the spirit and power of God. He fills us with the gift of who He is, thereby He may have a relationship with us, call us His children .being in His image. Because He is also a spirit, and they that worship Him, must worship Him in spirit and in truth, the only way to do that is by having His spirit inside, teaching us how to worship Him.

Friends, I want to share with you some of the other names of Jesus that are located within the Godhead of the Father. Yes, there are other names that honor Him. Please don't get confused when I say this. Nothing is more relevant than calling Him Jesus. By the name of Jesus, *all* knees shall bow and every tongue shall confess that He is Lord. At the name of Jesus, because of who He is, demons or demonic spirits will flee from you. That name, Jesus, is the source of our contentment and hope for all we do. Jesus is the name that we must use to get the Father's attention at the end of our prayers. His name is the epitome of power. Because of that name, we are free today. The One who shed His blood for us, Jesus! We can come boldly, but humbly (don't forget that), to the throne of grace and make our prayer requests known unto the Father.

In the next chapter, I have listed a few names of God for your studying. Remember, this is still Jesus. We have gone over the understanding of how the personalities work here and in another part of this book. I have described them as the names of Jesus. However, just in case you don't have access to references, I have taken the pleasure of doing it for you. Remember, all things good are done in the name, and that name is J*esus*. Remember, it's all about Him and your life, *After the Alter*. Amen.

10

WHAT'S IN A NAME?

Alpha and Omega	The beginning and the end	Revelation 21:6
Bread of Life	The one essential food	John 6:35
Chief Cornerstone	A sure foundation of life	Ephesians 2:20
Christ (Greek, Christos) literally the Anointed One)	This title makes clears Jesus' redemptive mission and affirms His fulfillment of Old Testament Prophecy	Matthew 16:16
God	The Father of All	Hebrews 1:8
High Priest	The Perfect Mediator	Hebrews 3:1-4, 14
Immanuel	The One who stands with us	Matthew 1:23
Jesus	His Personal	Matthew 1:21

(Yahweh)	Name	
King of Kings, Lord of Lords	The Sovereign Almighty	Revelation 19:16
Lamb of God	Offered His life as a sacrifice for sins	John 1:29
Light of the World	One who brings hope and gives guidance	John 9:5
Lord	Sovereign Creator and Redeemer	Romans 10:9
Mediator	Redeemer who brings sinners to presence of God	1 Timothy 2:5
Messiah	The tactile connecting the Old Testament prophecy with the New Testament of a coming Prophet, King, and Priest	John 1:4
Prophet	Faithful proclaimer of God's Word	Luke 13:33
Rabbi	Teacher of Scripture	John 3:2
Savior	One who	John 3:16

	delivers from sin and death	
Son of God	Deity, signifying Jesus' intimacy with God	Matthew 27:54
Son of Man	Identifying Jesus with us	Matthew 20:28
The Word	The communication of God to man from creation until now	John 1

There are many other names that are exclusive to your intimacy with Him. Again I wrote a few for your reading pleasure. These names are more personal to your relationship. These names are in the Hebrew form such as:

El-Elyon	The Most High God
El-Olam	The Everlasting God
El-Shaddai	The God Who is All Sufficient
Jehovah Tsidkenu	The Lord our Righteousness
Jehovah Raphi	Healer
Jehovah Jireh	Provider
Jehovah Shammah	With Me
Jehovah Rohi	The Lord our Shepherd
Jehovah Mekaddishkem	The Lord our Savior
Jehovah Nissi	The Lord our Banner
Jehovah Elohim	The Eternal Creator

These are just a snapshot again of the greatness of God, what will you call Him today? I don't know, but whatever you call Him, don't forget to call on Him as your only Lord and Savior that you may learn to live saved, holy, and free. John 8:36 quotes it as this, *therefore if the Son makes you free, you shall be free indeed;* and by all means don't forget to call Him…**JESUS.** Remember, it's the only name that makes the devil flee, *After the Alter* experience.

11

THE BLOOD

In this chapter, I wanted to write an in-depth thesis on this subject. However, the Father would not allow me to do so. He said, "Daughter, just give them the basics and I will give them rest as they go along." I obeyed.

Who has believed (confidently, trusted in, relied on, and adhered to) our message (of salvation)? And to whom (if not us) has the arm *and* infinite power of the LORD been revealed? For He (the Servant of God) grew up before Him like a tender shoot (plant), And like a root out of dry ground; He has no *stately* form or *majestic* splendor; that we would look at Him; nor (handsome) appearance that we would be attracted to Him. He was despised and rejected by men. A man of sorrows *and* pain and acquainted with grief; and like one from whom men hide their faces.

He was despised, and we did not

appreciate His worth *or* esteem Him. But (in fact) He has borne our griefs. And He has carried our sorrows *and* pains; yet we [ignorantly] assumed that He was stricken, Struck down by God and degraded *and* humiliated (by Him). But He was wounded for our transgressions, He was crushed for our wickedness (our sin, our injustice, our wrongdoing); the punishment (required) for our well-being *fell* on Him, and by His stripes (wounds) we are healed. All of us like sheep have gone astray, we have turned, each one to his own way. But the LORD has caused the wickedness of us all (our sin, our injustice, our wrongdoing) to fall on Him (instead of us).

He was oppressed and He was afflicted, Yet He did not open His mouth (to complain or defend Himself) like a lamb that is led to the slaughter, and like a sheep that is silent before her shearers. So He did not open His mouth. After oppression and judgment He was taken away; and as for His generation (His contemporaries), who (among them) concerned Himself *with the fact*. That He was cut off from the land of the living (by His death) for the transgression of my people, to whom the stroke (of death) *was due*? His grave was assigned with the wicked; but He was with a rich man in His death. Because He had done no violence, nor was there any deceit in His mouth; yet the LORD was willing to crush Him, causing Him to suffer; He would give Himself as a guilt offering (atonement for sin).

He shall see *His* (spiritual) offspring, He shall prolong *His* days, and the will (good pleasure) of the LORD shall succeed *and* prosper in His hand. As a result of the anguish of His soul, He shall see it and be satisfied; by His knowledge (of what He has accomplished the Righteous One), my servant, shall justify the many (making them righteous—upright before God), (in right standing with Him), For He shall bear (the responsibility) for their sins. Therefore, I will divide and give Him a portion with the great (kings and rulers), and He shall divide the spoils with the mighty, and because He (willingly) poured out His life to death; and was counted among the transgressors. Yet He Himself bore *and* took away the sin of many, and interceded (with the Father) for the transgressors. (Isaiah 53: 2-12)

If you study these passages of Scripture,

you will find everything that His blood brought us. If you need healing, it's in the blood. If you need deliverance, it's in the blood. If you need your mind restored, it's in the blood. If you want the devil to flee, you need to plead the blood of Jesus. If you want peace in your home, plead His blood. Every drop of blood that Jesus shed was for you and me. As the text says above, the chastisement of our peace was upon Him. The blood, as mentioned in other chapters, absolutely covers us, protects us and heals us. Remember, you have the right to this inheritance, this blood covenant through repentance and belief on Jesus, *After the Alter* experience. Amen.

12

BAGGAGE CLAIM

When my kids were approximately 3, 4 and 14 years of age, they loved to watch the planes take off at the Detroit Metropolitan or City Airports. Of course, like most children, they always had a lot of questions. Unfortunately, because I was not mechanically inclined, I could only answer a few. At that age, you know they think that you have the answers to all the questions they could think of; you're their hero. As time went by, they would find out that I certainly did not have the answers to all of their questions and that parenting is made up as you go along. Sure, I know there are many books written on parenting; however, because every household is different, every parent writes their own individual book in life…mentally.

You know other questions like, "Mommy, where do babies come from?" "Daddy, why do we have to go to school?" "Mommy, why is the sky only blue sometimes?" and "Do we live forever?"

"Daddy, why does Santa Claus only come at night?" Why this and why that? Those types of questions could go round and round and you try to get the answers they need; if you are a patient parent. My mother, however, would say, and I quote, "Stop asking me so many *blank-blank* (you can fill that in) questions and go do something with yourself." I didn't realize back then that it wasn't that she didn't want to answer the question. She simply didn't always know nor have the answers due to her limited education and lack of knowledge. After all, she was just a young woman with five children; practically still a baby herself. Remember when you thought your parents had all the answers, and you couldn't survive without them because every time you had a problem they always said the right thing to solve them? Maybe it was your parents; maybe an aunt, uncle, cousin, or even an older brother or sister. As life goes on, however, you realize that some issues will need to be solved by you. You also learned that your family was not always going to be there; not even your best friend for life. Trust, I know; I lost three in one year.

Not only did the kids enjoy the planes, they also were fascinated by the baggage area. We would go down to the baggage claim check just for fun. We watched all the baggage go round and round on the turntable or conveyor belt. We watched them come down one at time or sometimes at multiple times. Of course, if the baggage was not retrieved fast enough, we would see the same baggage go around again at least 20 times before someone would come to claim them. I am sure you've experienced at least one trip where you've had to take a plane or two. You can imagine the thoughts going through a child's mind as they watched the entire baggage come out of nowhere and end up somewhere, taking them by surprise every time. They were not aware at the time that there were people pushing the baggage through, and this was their job.

I was once a certified flight attendant and sometimes, things didn't always go as planned on a plane with the baggage or the passengers. As we very well know, there are different incidents and situations, that catches us off guard and if we're not careful, the issue will take us for an unexpected ride. Those same circumstances sometimes come with all types of turmoil waiting for us; but aren't you excited to know that nothing catches the Father off guard? As the pilots on a plane, if we have read our manuals (Bible), there is always a way of escape. There is only one we can look to when we go through these trials and tribulations. We look for those who say they love us, because they are your friend, sister or brother. But, I've found out that once you've received Jesus Christ as your Lord and Savior, the security of some of those loved ones sometimes... change. You didn't know that those relationships were predicated upon you staying as the old you; who you were, at that time. People are most comfortable around those who are just as they are, whether it's the high life or low life. When a change has come into their camp, or when you've moved on, especially become a part of God's family; they are offended. Because, although we need it, most of us don't like change nor do we welcome change.

When a Godly change has come over you, there is a difference! Those people speak the famous two words heard all over the world: "You've changed." When you are really striving to live for Christ, your response should be one of saying, "Good, that was the plan." In this walk, loved one, when you decide to no longer live the old you, but walk in the newly saved you, you will leave many behind. You have made a change in your life to follow Jesus. Then God has received you and truthfully, everyone is not happy for you; everybody is *not* celebrating the change they see in you. Most often the closest one to you will remind you of your past, as if you weren't there and are waiting for your demise. They will remind you of what you use to do and tell you to your face they will be watching you, because this will not last long.

Let me give you a few Scriptures on this to help you understand where I am going with this. In Matthew 12:46-49, while Jesus was teaching the scribes and the Pharisees, his mother and brothers began to look for Him. When He was told this, His response was as this, *"Who is my mother and who are my brethren?... For whosoever shall do the will of my Father which is in heaven, the same is my brother, and sister, and mother"*. He stretched out His hand and pointed at those who were gleaning from the words coming out of His mouth (His teachings). What are you saying? I am glad you asked. I am saying that on the road of salvation, you will lose those loved ones who are not ready to receive Jesus Christ as their Lord and Savior. I am saying; don't get discouraged, because most of your relationships were just as we spoke about earlier in this chapter: baggage. We didn't know it at the time, because we were riding with them round and round on the conveyor belt of life. Funny thing is that whenever you decided to get off the baggage wheel and/or no longer claim broken, raggedy bags, but shop for a brand new set of luggage (a better life), they should have gotten off too. However, they continued to ride life in a fog. Understand, you will always face opposition from those nearest you first; it's expected so don't be surprised.

I know right now you're probably feeling disappointed because you chose life. Don't be discouraged or dismayed; there's greater coming if you believe. You must learn to lean and depend on God for His love and His comfort. His Word says in Matthew 11:28, *"Come unto me, all ye that labor and are heavy laden, and I will give you rest. Take my yoke upon you and learn of me, for I am meek and lowly in heart: and ye shall find rest for your souls. For my yoke is easy, and my burden is light"*. A description of this Word would be a person who is a laborer, and is struggling with heavy burdens and is feeling overwhelmed by the work or load he or she was carrying.

A yoke is a double harness which two animals pulled together. Oftentimes, one harness was a larger one meant for the stronger, more experienced animal, while the smaller one was used for the weaker, inexperienced animal (a baby in this kind of work). The yoke of Jesus Christ is a much lighter burden to bear and He will never fail you. He says to take His yoke upon you and even says He will give you rest. Jesus is describing what happens when you put your trust and all things in His hands. This includes all of the baggage from your past: baby-mama/baby daddy drama, *I wish I knew then, what I know now* drama, *my mother didn't give me this or that* drama, *my life as a child was hard* drama, *my father didn't love me* drama; it's all relevant. However, it's all *baggage, baggage, baggage*.

He's offering salvation and a brand new life orchestrated by Him. He will strategically help you maneuver out of the web of the enemy's deception by teaching you His ways and pleading the blood of Jesus. I was once told that a person, who is a baggage handler, has a very stressful job and it is often difficult for various reasons. When everyone has turned their backs on you, God is able to send you brothers and sisters who will help you, love you, and build you up with *His* love and understanding. Now don't be fooled; there are some who have already been called to Christ that still have baggage and dwell in the midst of recovered baggage. But, if you draw closer to the cross daily (acknowledging Him in all your ways) God says that He will direct your paths.

You see, the Father is the only one who can change your baggage to luggage, a much lighter and easier load. It's easier because you will only bear what you're able to carry. He will carry the rest, carrying it along the way, as you get your breakthrough and rest in Him! He says to learn of me; get to know my ways and inquire of me, familiarize yourself with me and love me; I am gentle. He cares for you and nobody loves you like He does.

Along the way my friend, you will be astonished at those who will intentionally try to shake your peace in Jesus. However, I want you to remember, that it's not them, but the devil that uses them. He (the devil) is a divider and he will do all he can to attempt to embarrass the God in you. That's why you must wash your mind daily with the Word of God. You must study so that you will have the Word of God as your ammunition. As you wash your mind and pray daily, you will notice the unwanted baggage open up, unload itself, get lost and you won't find it anywhere in your spirit. I want to make this point right here: your soul got saved, not your flesh or mindset. It's up to you to work on both of those, through the washing and daily mediation of His Word.

Once you take flight in Him, you won't even notice the old you anymore. It has been replaced with love, patience, kindness, gentleness, meekness, which is described as *fruit of the spirit* in Galatians 5:22.The truth of the matter is that, friends will leave, but God will give you *"the peace which passeth all understanding, shall keep your hearts and minds through Christ Jesus"* (Philippians 4:7). He will never leave you nor forsake you. We might leave Him, but He won't leave us; He's always there.

Sometimes, it's better for us, people of God, to lessen our visits with family and friends until we can handle ourselves around them spiritually. The devil would love to tempt us with old habits and people once we have left the old baggage for newness in Christ. He would love to go to our Father and be the accuser of the brethren. They really are distractions to take us away from the presence of God. You really need those who are stronger than us to lead and guide like a pilot in training until we are ready to fly solo, because association truly does bring assimilation; whether it's good or bad! This simply means if you are seen with them, you are probably just as them. Be aware that sometimes you will never have the strength to be in the same company with "old friends." I know this may seem a little harsh, but let's go back and be reminded about Jesus, when He asked the question. "Who are my mother and my brother?" Jesus posed a question as if He were not familiar with them, with their character, nor their situations. Surely He knew His mother who had birthed and taken care of Him; surely He knew His natural father and His brothers; but Jesus was making a point.

If you're not walking in the same direction I am, then you are a hindrance to me. Only those who are seeking the will of My Father in heaven are worthy to be called my brother and my mother. Jesus was not saying that His parents or siblings were not doing the will of His Father; because, in essence, they were. Everything that was being done concerning Jesus was done that the Bible may be fulfilled in the Earth. I am not advising that you discontinue conversing with your loved ones. I am saying let your conversation be that of a blood bought and washed saved Christian. Change your conversation. Let your light so shine before men that they will see the new you, the Jesus in you, the hope of glory. If you don't know how to handle them, rely on God; He will lead you. Yes, in the world it is said, "Don't throw the baby out with the bath water. The meaning of this is don't get rid of the person just because they sit in dirt. Everybody can be made over or cleaned up again; get a fresh start. Please be mindful not to be arrogant in your new journey in God. I admonish you to always be courteous to those lacking in the faith so you don't cause them to stumble more. They may desire the God they see working through you. Win them by your conversation, love, and attitude in Christ Jesus. Jesus was not trying to disrespect relationships, and neither am I.

However, some are toxic and most toxic to the growth in our quest to walk in sanctification. You are not to allow that. Although they can see the baggage coming down on the conveyor belt, my children didn't realize that sometimes baggage gets lost and you might have to go to the Baggage Claim to reclaim that which was lost; like us. You see, we started out as baggage to God-lost and on our way to a burning hell. There's a saying that says, "Sometimes you can't go home again." This simply means that even though you have discovered who *you* are, some can't handle the *new* you, could care less about the *new you* and would rather not see the changed you...move on. Rest assured dear hearts, sometimes, in order to maintain this new life; you simply can't go back home again, to those people, places and things, you once knew. 2 Peter 2:21-22 says *"For it had been better for them not to have known the way of righteousness, than, after they have known it, to turn from the holy commandment delivered unto them. But it is happened unto them according to the true proverb, The dog is turned to his own vomit again; and the sow that was washed to her wallowing in the mire"*. Don't journey back to that same location and assume you are ready to live life as you did, because believe me, you will find things just as you left them (in disarray). Some will continue to wallow in their sins and if you're not careful, you'll be back in the (mire) mess with them.

Therefore, once you have tasted the goodness of Jesus and all of the things He's done for you, your heart will sing. Your friends and family won't always accept the revised you; you're under new management. Assuredly, I say unto you, don't disrespect who they are, because if it had not been for the grace of God, that could still be you. That was you and I. Your assignment now is to love them with the love of Jesus Christ, introduce them to Jesus and walk away in peace. Regardless of the baggage they may still carry, you know the Savior is love and that's how you love them, pass their flaws, falls and all. You don't throw the new found you in their faces, but you walk in His love and remember to share how His love and word delivered you from the baggage of sin that use to so easily beset you (that tripped you up all those years).

The Bible reminds us that you must be saved and living a lifestyle of holiness to be called the sons of God. I am reminded of words from a song that says, *this train is a holy train and bound for glory and the only way you can ride, you got to be holy.* There is a price for that holiness: repentance and separation! I'm reminded of Him also saying that those who do not give up everything to follow me, is not worthy of me (Luke 14:33).

Let's view another example. In Genesis 13 (paraphrased), one day, Abram prayed and asked God for help because he and his kinsmen (relatives) were not in agreement with one another, (spiritually and naturally). God told Abram to get up from where he was and *separate* himself from his kindred and go where

He (the Father) tells him. Once he was apart from them, God began to tell Abram all the blessings He (the Father) had in store for him, and that he would make his name great and that he was going to be a blessing to others.

So as I close this chapter, Abram could only see his baggage and he compared himself to kinsmen. In his eyes, they all looked the same. However, because God sees all, and knows all, they may look the same, but, oh how different the baggage really were. Each person's baggage is filled with many things, unto which may be harmful to you, but not them. Some baggage is a little heavier than others. Some baggage has treasures from years and years ago. Hear me. Some baggage have holes in them and unannounced to you, the contents are falling out. Which one fits you today? Everyone has baggage tucked away hidden in the back of their closet (heart and mind). It's time to open the closet and unpack that baggage, because you have become a hoarder of life's circumstances and God is calling on you to allow Him to unpack it for you. Unpack it by His love and peace. Some baggage is filled with things that you might die from, literally.

Everyone has their own baggage to carry to the altar. You see, I don't know where the Father found you in this life; saved or not. But, one thing I do know: Jesus came to reclaim that which is broken, damaged and lost amongst this age, and that's you and I. Allow Jesus to take the junk out of our trunks and replace it with treasures from heaven.

My sister, my brother, if you would leave from the abandoned place of despair where you are and go, the Father will make you a blessing for others and make your name great in the kingdom. Abram had to leave the place of familiarity to receive his blessing and hear the promises from an unfamiliar place. He needed to be in a quiet position within himself. The possibilities of where you will represent in God is endless.

In conclusion, brethren, my children did not know we were on our way to a burning hell, until the Father came to the Baggage Claim, and claimed us with His claim check marked with His blood, and turned us from baggage (abandoned /abused by life/ lost) into luggage (a more desirable valuable vessel for Christ), a gift to Himself. You see, my children didn't understand that although it seemed as if they could see all the baggage on the conveyor belt, there are smaller baggage tucked away inside under clothes that are only seen when necessary. They didn't realize that sometimes it gets lost and the owner will have to locate them. They didn't realize that sometimes the baggage can get left at the last location and the aspect of recovery is almost impossible. But, aren't you glad that the sheep herder left the 99 to get one sheep that was lost? The ones that were already there did not need him; the one that was lost was the most endangered species, amen.

Again, I don't know where the Father has found you today; no matter where; I am glad you're reading this book. Because right now God is saying, "Sons and daughters, this is your captain speaking, and we would like to accept your invitation to come onboard from Destitute Life to New Beginnings, Flight number 888. We will be leaving Misery Lane Airport momentarily, onto the city of Eternal Life, where we are expecting a fairly smooth ride; because you've decided to fly with us *After the Alter*, where all things change, even your name, address, and even how you live. There will be some turbulence; however, we are equipped to handle it. There will be times of uncertainty of weather, but we can handle that, too. We might go into a storm or two; however, I will carry you through, if you trust me as your pilot. Please take this time to say goodbye and fasten your prayer belts because when you fly with us, we move into lightning speed. We can handle all of your needs according to the riches and glory menu. So sit back, relax and enjoy the ride. You are now free to move about in joy and peace in the heavenly places, within the Holy Ghost. Thank you for joining us; this has been your Captain, Co-pilot and Flight Attendant, Jesus."

"But, I have prayed for thee, that thy faith fail not; and when thou art converted; strengthen thy brethren" (Luke 22:32). Therefore, let us stop by the baggage claim of the altar, so you can throw those grave clothes away so our God can give you beauty for ashes. You don't need those old clothes anymore! Father, I come as humble as I know how to throne of mercy and grace, laying down everything I am and everything I hope ever to be in You according the plans You have for my life…

You can take it from there.

Remember, to unload your baggage... *After the Alter!* Amen.

13

SWITCH BLADE

Whenever someone says, "Sticks and stones may break my bones; but words will never hurt me," they're lying and it's a cover-up. When the memorization comes from those *"words,"* it often brings pain. It's at that point you realize that the words spoken from your childhood until now actually, absolutely did and does still hurt you. The pain that stems from your inner core, the deepness of your soul; the real you, it affects your bones, causing a gnawing pain that eats through the bone down to the marrow (the substance of who you are). It which causes the flow of cortical, your body's stress hormone, to heighten as your heart beats faster each time you replay them in your cerebral cortex (mind) or hear those words spoken. Memory lane, I don't want to go there again.

Whether it's spoken from a loved one, friend or foe, it begins to bring back memories of the very first time the pain began. Many sticks and stones have literally broken many bones, from those in relationships or car accidents from driving away fast from a scene after someone said something hurtful. The memorization of those words can cause later problems in life. Studies have shown that children carry memories as young as six months old. Therefore, when they hear a certain sound, voice or experience, a certain physical pain occurs later in their lives. It takes them all the way back to when they first experienced it.

So, not only do the sticks and the stones break your bones, but this kind of pain cuts you like Zorro, leaving you with a Z on the front and the back of your soul with one swift movement. Words can leave a long-lasting impression on your mind; the pretty and the ugly. The right words spoken by the wrong woman can make a man melt like butter and become clay in her hands, as words from the wrong man can make a woman forget about her morals and become someone she'd never imagined she would be. However, right words spoken from the right person will make a man or woman soar like an eagle and grow to become great in the earth. Words spoken can make you steal, kill, and destroy. Sounds familiar?

Wait. Words that drip like honey from a person's lips can make you creep stay at home or make you cry all night long. I'm talking about *words*. Oh, how powerful they are! They can you make you better or worse. Words… let's move forward.

Words can sometimes determine the will of your desire to pursue your dreams and the ability to have what the world deems a normal relationship between two heterosexual people or the inadequacy of the same. Often, words said can derail and stifle a person's drive to perform in employment, family life and, here we go, even in sexual relations. Believe it or not, maybe it's you whose street I'm driving down right now. Words can keep a person from doing the daily activities of life, such as simply taking a bath. Tainted words can prohibit someone from making the right decision and the ability to hunger. Think about this the next time you see someone living under a bridge. This is sensitive, but real. The Father wants you to know that surely out of the heart truly flows the issues of life (Proverbs 4:23). Words can keep you from coming out of the cave of darkness and taunt you with paralyzing fear, and fear, my friend, is birth from darkness. Because we are now the light of the world, we should not display fear, only His light. *"God hath not given us a spirit of fear; but of power, and of love, and of a sound mind"* (2 Timothy 1:7).

You're probably thinking at this point, what this have to do with this chapter's title? Stay focused. Can we step back briefly to grade school, high school and for some of us, even college? All through school, the English and Language Arts teacher's job would be to help us understand words and the meaning of them. Not only was the meaning important, but the context in which you use 'these" words were most advantageous as well. Teachers would say, "You just can't go throwing words around; they'll land on something or someone to be effective." You can recall when you were a child, your mother would say, "Ok now, if you don't have anything nice to say, then don't say anything at all." This is why the Bible says that *"Death and life are in the power of the tongue: and they that love it shall eat the fruit thereof"* (Proverbs 18:21).

Words can rip through a heart, immobilize, and then break the bones (self-esteem), leaving a life for dead.

Guess what? Even if you have never gone to jail for it, if you are not encouraging someone with your words, but suffocating someone with your words; you are indeed a murderer. I have never killed anyone with my words, you're probably saying to yourself. Come now, I guarantee that you, I and everyone reading this book has killed a person or two with our mouths a time in our lives. Therefore, I'm going to help you get delivered. Get delivered from what? That almighty *Switch Blade...* your mouth!

Quickly, walk with me to Revelation Road to understand the effects of the Switch Blade. Incidentally, we may feel because a person did not tell us that we hurt them or because they did not die in front of you, we assume they are alright; not true. Just because you did not attend their funeral also doesn't mean they lived after communicating with you and I. Be honest; do you speak harshly every time a certain person comes around you? You may be saved; however, you continue to be rude and disrespectful to folks? If you agreed to this, you got something going on inside of you that need to be healed.

In passing, no one can even say hello to you, without you leaping down their throats, and all they said to you was "Good morning." That is not of God, don't be a nice-nasty saint and call yourself the salt of the earth. Is God pleased with that? You immediately pull out the blade. Let me say right here, as the spirit of God is leading me. The Bible says that *"The word of God is quick, and powerful, and sharper than any twoedged sword piercing even to the dividing asunder of soul and spirit, and of the joints and marrow, and is a discerner of the thoughts (character) and intents of the heart"* (Hebrews 4:12). The word of God is the only blade a person needs to see. Some preachers like to say this, "It cuts coming in and cuts going out." Well, this two-edged sword is God, because *"In the beginning was the word, and the word was with God, and the word was God"* (John 1:1).

The sword is the thoughts (logos) of God. That's why it's sharper because not only did His words land and make things appear, His words cut away at the darkness, and they landed and brought forth the earth and created a people. However, sometimes the words we bring forth become as a switchblade, harming, yet not healing. Then, we turn around and wanna bless God with that same tongue. James 3:10 says this should not be. When the sword of the Father goes in, He is surgically removing everything that is rotten and dead and prunes our soul branches so we may bear fruit and then more fruit (John 15). God's sword cuts straight through at the time of conception, to heal and deliver. But the sword that you and I use goes in and cuts from side to side, cutting away at every vital organ of the soul; not healing, but hurting. Our tongue, although it is a small member, it can cut hard and low. What we've said bears no fruit in anyone. A friend once mentioned to me that sometimes God should literally shut us up so that we don't mess people up.

This tongue can bear bitter, depressing and evil fruit not only in others, but in us as well. Our tongue is full of fire and a world of iniquity waiting to blow as a dragon in a children's story book. What we must do is turn the blade of God on ourselves and cut out all of the junk we've stored through lust of the eyes and the pride of life. Confess our faults, repent, speak life, and show love towards the people of God.

We must show love through our words one to another as we walk out this life of salvation. Trust me saints, someone is watching you. That's how this book got started. I know all too well that in this life, that sharp speech can be the result of pain, discouragement, depression, and again, disappointment. It is used as a shield due to some of our upbringings (childhood/relationships). Bitterness and the sharp tongue are accepted in your mind so that you don't succumb to trusting someone again. But, *you are "a new creature: old things are passed away; behold all things are become new"* (2 Corinthians 5:17). *The* "become" in this passage means, that every day as you walk in Him, you should be becoming new, allowing Him to strip you of the old ways and putting more of Him on; understanding that your soul was saved, not your flesh. Your spirit gets stronger daily, if you communicate with Him daily. This is why He reminds us to wash our minds daily *by letting this mind be in you, as it is in Christ Jesus* (Philippians 2:5).

The Apostle Paul also mentions not to allow corrupt communication be known amongst you once you have believed (Ephesians 4:29). He also says bad company corrupts good manners (or character) (1 Corinthians 15:33). You must let those things go in order to grow in God. Don't act or look surprised at this moment. Come on now, be honest. Are you corrupting someone or are they corrupting you? Whichever, this cannot be in Christ. If you are, ask the Father to put a hot coal on your tongue that you may only speak things that are pure and true (Philippians 4:8). Stop lying also.

My friend, allow me to remind you that death (corruption, malicious, lies, envy, strife, murder by words) and life (pure, honesty, pleasant, satisfaction etc.) is in the power (ability) of the tongue. Are you speaking life or death into your neighbor, your leader or your own situation? If you are a babe or even a seasoned saint, I admonish you to choose to speak life. We must kill our flesh with His Word daily in order to fight the inner us to keep the enemy from defeating us. We are blood bought and must seek to bear the fruit of the spirit that Paul talks about in Galatians 5:22-23. If we don't, the switchblade in our mouths will be so sharp, just sitting around waiting to be released.

You basically watch, stalk, and wait on someone to say something you deem a little disrespectful, so you can lash out. You live your life on the "I wish somebody would....I'll give them a tongue lashing they will never forget." Do you not know that a tongue lash brings on unwanted stress, anxiety, and always got you in a defensive mode. Truth is, if you would take the time in Christ to analyze it all, the person(s) is not necessarily the actual target. There is an internal situation going on within you; it needs to be identified. You have a stronghold working in your life. Deliverance is available at the altar. Believe me, it's the inner you. Your flesh is warring against the changes of God inside; it's diabolical! I want you to grab hold to a couple of things about the switchblade knife. Try to hear me with your spiritual ear.

The switchblade knife is equipped with a button on the side of it with a spring magnetism built into it. All one would need to do is push the button on the side and the spring will release the blade in seconds. Are you sitting around waiting for someone to push the right button, that you may release a wrath of evil on them? Or, are you surrendering your weapon of choice to God today? Truth is you should no longer desire the swirling of that blade in your mouth. I can see those invisible cuts on both sides of your mouth right now; looking as the Joker in the new *Batman* movie. It's dangerous to them and yourself. For a moment let me divulge this piece of information to you. Because the inner you is the enemy against you, we must also be aware of the words sown towards ourselves by ourselves. Sometimes, we can be our worst critic. It would be difficult for you to hear from the Father when you are sabotaging your own spirit and destiny.

In His own words, God says we are *"the head, and not the tail...above only, and not...beneath"* (Deuteronomy 28:13). He says we are *"fearfully and wonderfully made"* (Psalm 139:14). Shall I continue? Child of God, say what He says about you, to you. Build yourselves up in Him. We cannot say what the devil says and not what God says about us and expect to have a blessed soul. Whose report will we believe? We, even in the body of Christ, sometimes have lived on Sorrow Road between Doom and Gloom Street. We have no will, no tenacity to change lanes and drive around the corner to Self-Motivation Avenue. We don't visualize better, so we don't speak better. I hear the Word saying that we, as the church *"walk by faith, not by sight"* (2 Corinthians 5:7).

This brings me to this. I am an affirmations (words to speak over ourselves) fan. Within the last five years, I became an "affir-maniac" after being mentored by someone I call the "affirmations queen," Lady Crisette Ellis of Greater Grace Temple of Detroit. I had to stand in the mirror and talk to myself all the time because I was verbally abused for many years as a child and an adult. I had to find an outlet and then find the strength to leave. I hid this because I was a "preacher girl and a preacher's kid." I was involved in many ministries and I did not want my church family to really know what I was suffering. So, speaking affirmations were a way to get myself back. I could counsel someone to do better, restore marriages and even turn their lives around; however, I was not living in that specific victory myself. Back then, I was a fraud. I could speak motivation but wasn't living those words in private! Why? Because I was anointed to bring others out of the cave and yet did not have enough faith at the time to get out myself! If this is you living under the bondage of tongue lashing, seek help immediately! Save yourself!

Lady Crisette Ellis is the creator and founder of P.W.P, the Powerful Women of Purpose Ministries at Greater Grace Temple. She built P.W.P. on the premise of self-encouragement and self-examination to encourage women to look inside themselves to pull out gifts. Not only should we ask God what is their purpose; but, then we move and walk in those purposes/gifts. Lady Ellis began all of this with affirmations (words of love to one's self). If you are a man reading this book, you need encouragement, too. Speak over yourselves. Women love to be around the flow of a positive, confident gentleman. We enjoy seeing the energy of a man that can not only generate positive energy in him, but rescue others to do the same; so speak, *man*, speak! Lady Ellis encouraged us every Sunday morning with words of love, some owned-some borrowed. This went over so well with the women and men of grace, that she was able to launch her own affirmations clothing and accessories line. This includes, but not limited to, bookmarks, cards and bracelets. Her affirmations line has floated all around this country, and has empowered men and women to take their power back from the devil by speaking the Word over their lives. I would say that Lady Ellis is definitely using her tongue to speak life and empowerment to others; she is a Powerful Woman of Purpose.

As a mentalist, I discovered during studying and counseling others, that if they had an outlet to get the "pain" out, that the words of death and defeat would not come out that way. There are things in "me" that need to come out. This is their confession…and ours. We must stop making excuses for the harshness of our words. We think it's alright, but it's not. When you allow God to renew your mind, not only will the body follow, so will your words. Another thing: the Holy Ghost is a teacher; therefore the Lord will say, "Now son or daughter, you could have said that differently or in my love." Again, as saints, we cannot and should not use our titles as an excuse to be rude to others. Everything as much as possible should be done in love, even discipline or correction.

Stop saying you cannot control what comes out of your mouth. Read the entire third chapter of James. This chapter mentions how *men can tame everything from beast to boat and so forth; but his tongue he will not tame.* Is it that we can't, or that we won't? God is that source. I beseech you now to consider the phrase, "I can't." If we can control our tongues (and attitudes) when we communicate with our bosses, teachers, mothers, and pastors, equitably, the Lord is saying, we can control what we say to our spouses. Yes, I am all in your business because this is where the Father wanted me to go. His sons and daughters are crying out before Him because of this problem in Christian and non-Christian homes alike. Don't say you can't; you simply just won't. Dismantle and disarm the verbal and physical abuse in your homes. It is a spirit and it's from the devil. You need to really go back to the altar and then after the altar, return to your loved one for an apology and work through the root of the problem together.

No one is saying just because you are a servant, that you should be abused. However, Jesus was the example in turning the other cheek (Matthew 5:39). I know you are not a doormat and the Father is not asking you to be that. He is saying do everything in His name, in His love. God says, *"a soft answer turns away wrath"* (Proverbs 15:1a).We need to follow His words (commandments) to *"live peaceably with all men"* (Romans 12:18) this starts with bridling your tongue. When I was a child, I did not hold my words back. It was on my mind, then immediately out the mouth for me. No filter at all. This has been since I could talk. This is a true story. My mother had a terrible nickname for me, "motor mouth." If I wasn't singing, I was talking. My mouth was always moving, even in school. I always got in trouble with teachers and other students because of my responses to their words or conversation with me. Hear this; I grew up in a non-Christian home, so you can just imagine the stuff that was coming out of my mouth. I was my mother's child. Most of the time, at my mother's house, we only did church music on Sundays; that was our church.

However, I started going to church on my own with an elementary and middle school friend around 8 years old. I was leaving somewhat of a hell and entering heaven every Sunday, and I was glad. I learned of God's goodness early on while attending Greater Grace Temple of Detroit. But, my mouth was still following the flow of home. I would still slice and dice you up like a pizza without an apology at a young age. I didn't realize I was the offspring of a Pentecostal family and pastor that's another book).This explained the constant need to express my opinion, but not the excuse for a sharp tongue. That was a learned environmental behavior which once I came into the knowledge of God; I sought to change. I learned that my words hurt because I was hurting and I perpetuated the same household behavior.

Only God can change that tongue from speaking curses and cussing (if you are willing) to praise and worship. I loved people, I just was not taught to know what love looked like or how to speak through it.

You too, are a part of the tongue of murderers, slanderers and "Zorro clan." I hope at this point, you are choosing to walk in peace and change from tongue murder to speaking miracles. You can do all things through Christ because you are more than a conqueror; therefore, in closing, if you don't like the world you see, change what you say and then you will change what you see. God spoke what He wanted to see and He says that you and I can have the same power if we are in Him. Remember, you shall have, what you say! Remember, *your* words have power; practice speaking life ....*After the Alter*. Amen.

14

HOLE IN MY POCKET

Well, well, well. I believe we have come to a part of the book that people stand around the water cooler for, debating about who's right, who's wrong and whose business is it anyway. Hold on to your seat; this chapter is going to be a bumpy and candid ride. I imagine that I may step on a few more toes and possibly get an Amen or two from the pew warmers, as well as pastors who may be reading this chapter. I believe that I heard a word or two from the Lord about the tussle in the giving of tithes and offerings. This is entering the Father's nostrils as a sour and rotten smell. For all of you who are really hungry for an answer on this subject, please pay close attention and hear by the Spirit of the Lord that you may be in the will of the Father. So we're going to get right to the facts. In the event that you don't agree with my findings, I pray you are mature enough to say, "Hallelujah" anyhow.

Malachi 3:10a states, *"Bring ye all the tithes*

into the storehouse, that there may be meat in mine house". Let's stop right there. For all of you who don't understand why this text says "my house," this represents the church. You are included in that if you are a saved by grace and blood washed saint. Not the place that God currently dwells, but the church that you are a member of, perhaps you visit on Sundays, wherever you decide to drop by. Whether you are a seasoned saint or a C.M.E. (Christmas, Mother's Day, and Easter churchgoer), the text says to bring the entire tithes and offerings into the storehouse. The storehouse was a place in the Old Testament that animals and produce were stored to support the Levite priests and their families and others in the communities. Now the Israelites were apprehensive about doing this because of selfish reasons.

Now we know that the churches of today do not store animals and produce for the pastors and such. So naturally in our times, He's speaking of finances. If the lights are on in your local service, it's from the tithes and offerings. If there is heat on in the winter and air (electrical fans or otherwise) on in the summer at your service, that is because of the tithes and offerings. If there is a roof over your head at the church house, it's the tithes that did that. If there is running hot and cold water at your local assembly, it is done with the offerings. If you are in need at your home and the pastor obliges, thank the church for tithes and offerings. If your loved one has passed on and the family doesn't have the means for a funeral service, thank the church; because that's from the tithes and offerings being stored in the *storehouse*.

I want to let you know that it takes finances to spread the Gospel. Although salvation is free, it costs to feed the needy, cloth the naked and shelter the poor. The tithe is expected from everyone; God commands it. Beloved, the tithe is not for Him, it's all about you, that you may have the promises of the Father in its fullness. In the next verse of the text, it goes on to say, *"...try me now."* He's saying at that point to watch and see, trust me; for I am not a God that should lie. According to your faith, I will turn blessings your way immediately by opening the windows of heaven and pouring out blessing you won't have room enough to receive. This means that you'll have a constant flow of blessings when you give unto the storehouse in obedience.

Now listen, let's have a quick Bible class for those critiquing the word where God says, "I will pour you out a blessing, (this seems to be a single blessing but it is not) you won't have room enough to receive." This is because there are many blessings wrapped in that one. Malachi 3:8 states that man has robbed God of tithes and offerings. The Father clarifies this there because He wanted the nations to know why the curses will be so great. Let me clue you in on something. The tithes are different from the offerings. They are not the same. If they were, the Father would not have mentioned the two separately. The tithe is the tenth of all of your increase. The meaning of tithe is described as the tenth or ten percent of your increase.

Now on to the offering piece of this subject. You're going to be happy at the end of this chapter when I bring it all together from the opinion of the Father. The offering that you give to your local assembly is up to you. The Father did not give a specific amount to the Israelites and neither does He give it to us. God says to give according to your heart; listen to it. If you're still not convinced that you should be participating in the tithe and offering portion of the service, read on. The Father says in the continued text that in your giving, He *"will rebuke the devourer for your sakes"* (Malachi 3:11). Notice that it's for your name sake, not His. This is because He owns the cattle on a thousand hills, He doesn't need our money.

Wait.... there's more! After that, the Father has the audacity to say that I will rebuke him (the devil) so that the devil will not destroy the fruit of your ground. When was the last time you gave in church? When was the last time you decided that those shoes or that dress or cable bill was worth you being cursed with a curse? The curse is not in the lack of money. But the curse starts in your mind and then moves into your understanding.

Okay, pay attention. The first curse means that you are thinking in the wrong mindset when it comes to giving. The second curse means because you have set in your heart not to give, your monies are cursed. So therefore, that word of being cursed with a curse means that. You're cursed because of your thinking (or heart is blinded) then your monies are subject to never having enough because you won't give and your hand is closed. So if your hand is always closed, you can never receive anything in return; cursed with a curse. Selah.

Back to verse 8. *"Will a man rob God...?"* We are robbing Him if we're not giving tithes and offerings. Giving is a commandment; you make the choice. He's only asking for the little ten percent that really doesn't belong to you anyhow, *"...the earth is the Lord's and the fullness there of..."* (1 Corinthians 10:28b). I will also remind you that the Word of God tells us in Matthew 6:24, *"No man can serve two masters: for either he will hate the one, and love the other; or else he will hold to the one, and despise the other. You cannot serve God and mammon"* (money), it is enmity unto God. Beloved, if you feel as if tithes and offerings you have belongs to you and you're not giving the ten percent due to some bad advice, ask the Father for clarity! If you're not giving because you heard some preacher, who has not rightly divided the Word of truth, tell you it is a choice, read The Book of Life (The Bible). Maybe you feel that there are some Old or New Testament technicalities. Question, what would you do if the Lord decided that because of a technicality, He will only allow you to breathe ten percent? Will you give then? Maybe He'll allow you to only walk, talk, or eat ten percent; will you give then? Is it really worth holding on to those pennies?

If the government gets their way, pennies won't even have any worth; and to some, they are worthless anyway. When I say the tenth, I'm speaking from your gross amount, not the net. For God is not to be mocked. The Word reminds us that whatsoever a man soweth, that shall he reap; remember the "eth" means, continually. Giving your offerings consistently and cheerfully unlocks the doors of giving back unto you. It unleashes a spirit of favor upon your life. I promise, you will walk in a spirit of prosperity, people will run to give all things to you and they won't know why. This is the favor of God. I want to express to you as the Bible has in Deuteronomy 28:2, *"And all these blessings shall come on thee, and overtake thee, if thou shalt hearken unto the voice of the Lord thy God"*. In Genesis 2:16-17, it talks of God speaking to Adam, *"And the Lord God commanded the man, saying, Of every tree of the garden thou mayest freely eat: but of the tree of the knowledge of good and evil, thou shalt not eat of it: for in the day that thou eatest thereof thou shalt surely die"*. Now this next statement might rattle a few theologians; however, remember we agree to disagree. After all, we will not know all things until we meet the Book face to face.

Now it has been said traditionally that Adam and Eve died spiritually because they ate of the tree that the Father said not to eat from. Therefore, they were disobedient. It's also been often said that if Adam had not eaten the fruit at his wife's request, they would not have fallen because the commandment was given to Adam, and not Eve. However, I want to go a little further. Of course, I am not denying any of those things because they are correct. On the other hand, could it also have been because the Father set that tree aside for His usage and that it was a tithe given to Himself for Adam and Eve? After all, the Father required ten percent before the foundations of the earth. Chew on that for a moment.

He requires that we set aside the tithes and offerings before we do anything else. He wants His off the top. You may have noticed that both, tithes and offerings, have an "s" on the end of it. This means that we are to be consistent givers. Now beloved, I believe that the tree is a symbol of the tithes, a call to the order of God. In Genesis, again Abraham gave the tithe to the high priest of God, Melchizedek, along with an offering and did not take any for himself. Understand, precious, that The Word tells us in 2 Corinthians 9:6-7, paraphrased, that he who sows weak will also reap weak and he who sows great shall receive or be blessed greatly; therefore, give much that you shall receive much.

The Word says that God loves a cheerful giver. If you're giving but in your heart you do not "feel" comfortable or you give grievously, keep it. I say this because God knows your heart and He'd rather you give out of a loving heart instead of give as if somebody's robbing you as you have robbed Him. Giving tithes and offerings is worship unto God. Brethren, I want you to keep this in mind. Cain also gave grudgingly and the Father did not accept his gift because he gave it with not only the wrong heart, but after he took the better portion first, he gave the Father the leftovers. A good man will give his natural father the best that he has first, and then take the leftovers. A good man will do this because he loves and respects his father. We disrespect our Father when we hold back what belongs to Him; the tenth. If you're tussling with this, again I say, keep it. He doesn't want or need it, beloved.

Moving forward, we are now at the most exciting part of this chapter; revelation knowledge. For the seasoned giver who understands the principle of giving, but the fruit that is returned does not seem to match that which was given, I have an answer. We all understand that really you can never beat God's giving. It's not just a cliché. It's the truth and the truth God surely loves. I know sometimes it seems although you're giving, you're still in lack. Well, there's an answer to that question in mind. For so long in my mind, I struggled with that exact thing. It's simply because the Bible says that you will have what you say. It also says that you will reap what you have sown. Think back, we spoke of two important principles: say and sown. Many of you are saying at this very minute, I pay my tithes faithfully and give my offerings cheerfully, but we still seem to be vacant in our needs. We still can't seem to get ahead. There always seems to be more bills at the end of the month than money. Let me also dispel the myth, "you don't *pay* your tithes, you *give* your tithes." We all know, and I don't care how spiritual you are, no one and I mean no one enjoys paying bills, rich or poor. The tithe is not a bill. As mentioned, The Word says that God loves a cheerful giver, so we are to give with joy and expectation in our hearts, believing that God is going to return it multiplied. We always pay our bills grudgingly, knowing that if we don't pay them, we will be homeless, naked, hungry, etc.

It is also very important that you are a good steward over what is left after you have given. In the world of agriculture/farming, there are principles that must be adhered to in order to see a seed produce. Here are a few basic steps:

1. You must turn over the soil you are planting in. There must be a preparing of the land.
2. You must put holes in the areas you wish to plant, approximately one foot apart depending on your seed or your intended harvest. You do this so the

seeds do not entangle with one another as they began to grow.
3. Plant your seed and label each planted seed hole with the seed packet on a stick.
4. After all of the seeds have been planted, you must apply water to them and as they grow, make sure to weed around them to keep the weeds from killing the seeds or chocking the growth. Wait for the complete harvest of the seeds. You may only plant one seed, but many plants will be produced from that one seed.

What are you saying woman of God? Let's go there spiritually.

You must cultivate the land that the seed will grow in, that's you. You are planting the tithes in your land (symbolically), in yourself. Righteousness plays a part in this. Although the Word says to bring all the tithes into my storehouse, remember you are preparing seeds to be used, given and distributed however the church's administration sees fit. Before a tithe is even sown, you have purposed in your heart to give it, for you have already set it aside.

First, you have already prepared the soil

with praise and worship, reading and studying your Bible and spending time with the Father in prayer and fasting. However, there are other steps that must be taken. Secondly, you must name your tithes (this is not a "name it and claim it," but tell it what it will be). Every seed that you have planted, The Bible says you will have when spoken out of your mouth. When the tithes you have planted come up, you will know it by name because you called those things that are not, as though they were, by faith. Lastly, if you don't say it, then believe it, you won't receive it.

Yes, I know there is a touch of controversy going on in the hearts of men. Therefore, let me break this down a little further for you. If you plant the seed by faith, you must name it before giving it in offering that day. How dare you wait for your pastors to pray over *your* seed before you do? He/she doesn't know what to name it. I recognize that there are the five-fold gifts working in the ministry; however, nobody knows your needs better than you and God. Buckle up, here it goes. After you've prayed, planted (spiritually through prayer), brought it to church, given it, and your pastor prays over it again (watering it with agreement), God then will add the increase. Ok, I know you're not convinced that the woman of God is correct. Listen, I've worked these principles. Once I came into the understanding of how the Word of God works concerning this, I don't lack if I believe. All my needs are met every time. Proverbs 4:7b says *"with all thy getting get understanding"*. I dare you to take this word and try it. Send me an email! When you speak to it, you have told it what to produce (remember you've named it) so it will come forth as you named it.

There are more pieces to this puzzle the Father wants me to speak of, and it's this. When you tithe without commanding it, it's as if a farmer decided to plant seeds one day by just throwing them up in the air and allowing them to come down, hit the soil, and come up without knowing what he has planted. In other words, if you are waiting for a need to be met, but you have not commanded or spoken a word over your seed, yes it will come back as a blessing to you, but as what? I agree all blessings from God are great, but when you have an immediate need, you need an immediate seed. The tithe is for immediate needs, just as the priest needed in the Old Testament. Is this making sense? The Priests and their families couldn't wait for the members of the temple to procrastinate on bringing God their first fruits because the priests needed to take care of the needs of the church, which weren't limited to those of widows and the poor. What if you have a situation that arises, and you've already given the tithes and offerings that week? What do you do? You remind the Father in prayer. Remind Him that in faith you tithed and gave, and that you depend on Him for all your needs according to His Word. His Word instructs us to put Him in remembrance of His promises unto us; such as never seeing the righteous forsaken nor his seed begging bread. Remind Him of the promises He made to you. Remind Him how He fed the 5,000 and surely, if He did that for them, He is well able to do that and more for you. The Father takes pleasure in hearing you remind Him of His goodness and mercy. He loves hearing you speak His Word back unto him with faith, that's how you move God on your behalf. He is truly a rewarder to those who diligently seek His face. Yes, we are still talking tithes. Here's another thing I want to convey to you.

Just as the people gave unto the Priest a bullock, or a lamb, they could only use those animals for meals that required that type of meat. When giving of your tithes, you cannot take a tithe for one week and call it three things. In other words, if you were paid a one-week pay check, you only pray one thing over that tithe. Now back to the farmer. When a farmer plants a lettuce seed and it begins to produce, he is not looking for that seed to produce cabbage or carrots; it can't, it's just a lettuce seed. If the farmer desires carrots and cabbages, he has to sow for cabbage and carrots. Each week or bi-weekly that you receive your increase, you must speak to each tithe and tell it what to grow as. You cannot call one tithe several things in one Sunday. I hope that makes sense.

Now let's discuss the offering. The Bible says to give cheerfully. Again, there's no required amount on offering. I want to show you how the offering piece works. People of God, we have, for so long, been repeating the words, principles, and clichés of our forefathers that we assumed was in the Word, when in actuality, they aren't. Although I honor them, I have come to understand that they only repeated what they heard from their spiritual mothers/fathers without rightly dividing the word or studying themselves. I have even come to know that some sayings were just passed down through many generations and were thought to have been in His Word. We bless God for the mothers/fathers because they are the reason we are here today. We shall never forget how far we've come, because of so many great men and women of God; we are standing on their shoulders. Amen.

I once heard a wise man say, "You only know what you know and God's grace is sufficient." I wrote all of that to get to these points that follow: the offering you give is up to you. The Bible has no clear amount, it just says to give and I (the Father) will give it back to you in good measure, pressed down, shaken together running over, will men pour into your bosom; for with the same measure that you use, it will be measured back to you (shall men pour into your bosom).

In talking about the ground, Malachi 3:11 says that the Father will rebuke the devil for your sakes, so that he (the devil) will not destroy your ground that the fruit you planted (tithes and offerings) will not produce. In other words, the Father will rebuke the devil when you, in obedience and faith that is so relevant, give your tithes and offerings. The Lord will block the hand of the enemy so that he will not pluck up that which you have planted. The devil cannot cause confusion and fear by telling you that you will be in lack because you gave. He is a liar and the father of lies. God will bring forth a harvest, because through obedience and faith, the devil can't do anything but watch it grow when you are obedient to God's Word, thereby keeping your ground (seed) from being eaten. Did you know that through obedience in your giving, you will break the back of Satan's plans against you each time you give? Just as farmers use pesticides and such to prevent bugs and animals from ruining the crops, we use the Word of God to keep the devil away for a season. Yes, that joker will come back just like bugs and try again. But because we have the Greater One in us to speak the word, it sets up a pesticide wall against him.

I am reminded of the Pac-Man game (of which I am an avid player who happens to play very well). As you know, the game consists of you chomping all the little white dots before the ghosts chomp on you. Just as the devil, he and his imps are always trying to find a hole in your salvation to trip you up... But God! He's always trying to destroy your vine, before it's able to bear fruit... But God! If you are obedient, God will fight your battles.

I am not a person who sows discord in the Body of Christ, but I must be obedient to the voice of God by putting the things in this book that are necessary for God's people to be free and live an abundant life on earth, as the Father desires for us.

In my conclusion, I want to speak to those who emphatically and simply refuse to participate in the tithes and offerings part of the service. I also want to minister to those who are just not sure and have had so many different opinions spoken in the past; you have no idea what to believe. The Word says that God will rebuke the devil from your ground and from your vines, protecting you from your seeds being plucked up. Beloved, the giving of your offerings causes the blessings of finances over your life. The angels who know you by name will begin to work when you give your tithes and offering in faith. They also have names attached to them such as: mercy, miracle, protector, and healer. These are just some of the names given to them by God, to step in when they hear the word of faith coming forth out of your mouth.

Quick Review:

Tithes are for immediate needs (including financial). Offerings cause financial overflow. To those who are of the cloth, and you're enjoying the over flow of financial blessings in extraordinary leaps and bounds, it's because you are a *giver*. Keep it up! God is pleased with you. If you're a member and experiencing the same, keep it up! The Father is surely pleased and as long as you are a strong giver, He will give it back to you a hundred fold. Whatever measure you give, the same measure is given back to you in abundance. The Father opened my eyes and this word illuminated in me: we must rightly divide the word, so that we'll be able to teach others as God has called us to do. Just in case you might be one who's not going to give, well it's a choice you will live with and your needs will be met sparingly; as you have given.

Brethren, there is one more area that needs to be covered concerning tithes and offering: *marriage*. Because God is a God of order, all things must be in order to reach your full potential of the exceedingly, abundantly and above of what you can ask or think. 1 Timothy 3:5 says, *"For if a man know not how to rule his own house, how shall he take care of the church of God?"* I am speaking about order. If you are giving tithes and offerings and are in discord with your spouse, you are holding up the blessings in your household. I am by no means saying that the Father will not allow blessings to come. He can't go against His own spiritual laws or His own promises towards us. However, you will be blessed sparingly because your house is out of order, just as the non-tither. If you're giving, but hiding money from your spouse and you two have agreed to be accountable to one another financially, again you are out of order. You may think you're blessed in abundance, but you're not. The Father has been speaking to you on why the struggle is so great, but you are not adhering to His voice. Be open and honest with one another. If you have any faults with your spouse, come together and forgive one another. Watch the blessings pour out of the windows of heaven like rain. Believe me, this works! I have been there, done that and bought a few chastisement paddles to prove it.

Beloved, one of the tricks of the enemy is to get you and your spouse to be at odds, to shut down the flow of blessings from you. If he can distract you with foolishness, you're not able to not only hear your spouse's voice, but you can't hear God's voice either. He wants you to continue to trust in the Word and not the world. If you're still dealing with haters, naysayers and doubters of the Word of God in respect to tithes and offerings, you know the kind that says, "I ain't giving my money to no Bentley driving, Mercedes driving, Escalade driving stealing preacher." Try this principle and tell them to watch God work suddenly in your life. If they continue to be mouth draggers concerning the church by saying all they (pastors) want is my money and they're pimping the people, I would first say, get away from them; they're cursed. But, before you do, hit them with this. How many times have they gone to the church to ask the preacher for help with paying a light bill? They were prostituting the church. Paying the gas bill? They were prostituting the church. How about their rent? They were trying to *pimp* the church. How many times has the church assisted their loved ones with situations, including getting your loved one(s) out of jail? Think about it. They were trying to pimp the church/preacher, just as the lost pimped Jesus for bread, healing and delivering. Ask them how many times they have made false promises to God saying, "Lord if you get me out of this, I won't do *it* again?" Tell them that *they* were trying to pimp God, but He knows the intent of a man's heart. Those are the type of people, after the preacher has given from the storehouse of the church and helped them get on their feet, will try and tear down the character of the preacher, and crucify the church with their words. As the people also did to Jesus; some were only there for the fish and loaves.

When I think about the scripture of bringing all the tithes into the storehouse, during that time period, the job of the priest was to solely teach, encourage and pray for the people 24 hours a day, seven days a week, 365 days a year. Now, we are not living in those times. Pastors of today are judges, doctors, lawyers, presidents of companies and have plenty of stock, investments, etc., to live on. They are not standing at the church doors asking for alms, as you suppose. They have families and many other obligations than just the church. Here's an idea. Has anyone ever asked some of the world's most high profile rappers and superstars what are they doing with my $175.00 or more ticket monies? Has anyone ever asked a movie star what happens to the $15.00 ticket for the movie? Has anyone ever asked them does my money afford you to live in that mansion or drive that Rolls Royce? I think not. Yet, we scrutinize the man and woman of God, who holds the bread of life in their spirits and mouths; those who God has chosen to spread the Gospel that you may live again.

The media prosecutes and persecutes the televangelists and preachers for acquiring the things of the world as if we all should live in a hut; that's foolishness. If the world, which according to the Bible, will go to hell shortly, can enjoy the material things of this world, why can't the godly enjoy material things as well? God says that He came that we may have an abundant life. He is not just talking about after the rapture, but about here on earth as well. Another thing I am reminded of is 3 John 1:2, *"Beloved, I wish above all things that thou mayest prosper and be in health, even as thy soul prospereth"*.

Remember, God is not mocked. He says if you don't give it, you will be cursed with a curse, and that you'll have a hole in your pocket. This means that monies will seem to disappear no matter how you try and save it. It blows away as the wind. I think right about now, your heart should be ready to repent and ask for forgiveness due to the robbery that's in progress. This is a 911-emergency. Release the grease so that you will be free to give, *After the Alter*. Amen.

15

BODY PARTS

....but is this flesh, not more than a cell for the soul; a far greater prize?

Author Unknown

When we were birthed out of our mothers' womb, as early as kindergarten, we were taught and constantly reminded to keep our hands to ourselves. Not only our hands, but our eyes (don't roll them), our tongues (don't stick them out at anyone) our noses (cover when sneezing, please). And most certainly, we, as children were taught to keep our hands (don't touch those who don't want to be touched). There is no fighting, punching or pushing down of others! We must play nicely with our friends.

These things mentioned are known in the scientific world, as our senses. Our senses allow us to learn how to protect ourselves in the world, while enjoying ourselves in this same world. The senses usually work together to give us a clear picture of the things around us. If one sense is not working due to an accident or illness, then other senses will take over or become stronger to make up for the missing sense. For instance, many do not know that although like most, I have two eyes; however, I only have full vision in one of my eyes. No one has ever known that I cannot see out of my right eye. Strangely, my vision is stronger in one eye than that of most that have sight in both.

Our sense of sight is all dependent upon our eyes to see. Of course as Christians, if the Holy Spirit resides in us, we have natural and spiritual sight. The retina is covered with two types of light sensitive cells called the rods and cones. The rod, not only guides us naturally, but also comforts us according to Psalms 23. It allows us to see better at night naturally and spiritually in the dark times and places in our lives. The cones allow us to see colors, again first natural and then spiritual (joys of rightness or unrighteousness). These also aid us in our peripheral vision, naturally again and spiritually, (i.e. being able through prayer and discernment to see the attack of the enemy from the sides and back of us). This will all make sense soon. I am writing to you concerning our natural senses and am paralleling it with the spiritual as we go.

The information above is sent to the brain (cerebral cortex) which was mentioned in another chapter. I will tell you why it is so important to monitor what comes through your eye gates. We all see and process images every day, whether we are awake or sleeping. However, before we made Jesus the Lord and Savior of our lives; we were walking around dead with our eyes wide open. Being alive in Him gives us the images that are called *open visions*. However, when we are asleep, these are called *dreams*.

Let's speed up here. Our adversary will send visions to plant an image or he will speak a thought that will manifest into imagery by repetitive meditation. Images planted by the devil are always of self-promotion and self-gain. They are usually prideful, sexual and of selfish imagery. These images are sent usually through the entrance of the eyes and then planted in the mind which attaches itself to the soul and brings thoughts of flesh-pleasing imaginations.

Those thoughts are called fiery darts (Ephesians 6:16). Fiery darts are thoughts sent by the devil to throw you off course when you present your bodies to be beaten, bruised and then used for the will of God. The devil will bring forth thoughts and images from your past to set you up for failure. What you process and meditate on in your brains becomes the plot to take you back to the bondage you came from after repentance. The brain also uses those same images from two eyes or "one" eye to cause a 3D (three dimensional) image. This allows us to perceive what our spiritual depth is, to perceive what is false or real.

Our ears give the ability to hear in two separate parts. First, the outer ear retrieves the sound waves and transmissions as sounds pass by our heads. Secondly, the inner ear translates the vibrations into sounds to record and passes the message of those sounds to our brain through our auditory nerve. The brain then uses this to determine where the sound is coming from, whether it's on the right or left side of us. Now, because you and I have decided to become a part of the kingdom of heaven, these are areas that should always be on high alert to discern the voice of God and the attack from the enemy. We hear the voice of God from our spirit to our ears. The devil uses these senses to pervert what we see, hear, and believe; these things will be important to know again for the point of this chapter.

Our sense of taste comes from the taste buds on our tongue. Everything you taste is one or more combinations of these four senses flavors. As we have the natural where withal to taste foods. We also have the capabilities to desire and taste sin. We can almost taste the sin we crave; even after our altar experience.

Sometimes we hunger for certain sins or feelings such as the touch, feel and even taste of someone. Let's be grownups! To be held, touched, kissed or even the ultimate penetration of a lover. Don't look shocked about that statement; you know by now this book is candid and we must be transparent to get and continue in deliverance. The pleasure of touch is spread throughout the whole body and then connects to the brain waves which give signals to our nervous system, which makes us nervous and anxious. There are four kinds of touch sensations that can be identified: cold, heat, contact, and pain. Because we are blind to the cunning plans of the devil, we must use our sense of hearing through prayer when it comes to bumps in the road. His intentions are to trip us up on this thing of "feeling so good," that we forget about our commitment to God. He will do this by sending the right person, well, really the wrong person, to stimulate our emotions. He does this to interrupt our lifestyle through a series of stimulates. It begins with the stimulation of communication. Again, he will send someone to you when you "feel" at your lowest point of loneliness to awaken your natural senses (sight, hearing, smell, taste and touch) and all of these are sources of communication. These things are dead in Christ at the beginning of your walk. But can be awaken, if allowed, by inappropriate stimulations.

It's all a distraction! The purpose of that distraction is to begin communicating with someone you can see, hear, smell, taste and touch. I know this seems redundant; again it's vital to this chapter. You can get so wrapped up in talking with a physical person, that you forget or lessen the communication with God who has a voice, but no face. This is called deception by communication. Now you may think that there is nothing wrong with communicating with a person of the opposite sex; and you are right. However, during the course of communicating with this person, they are not just speaking with your ears, they are communicating with the other four senses of your being. Because we are human, what we internalize begins to cause us to fantasize or bring thoughts in the beginning not warranted, but then we begin to enjoy those thoughts after continuous communication with them. Those thoughts began to "touch" our lives which always results in the touching of our skin, our bodies. Now this begins the awakening of our nervous systems; those are the systems that make us feel feelings underneath our skin.

This person(s) has awakened our feelings which were once dead in Christ but are now alive again to the things of the world through communication. We are spirit, but we are flesh, also. This flesh always seeks to please itself first. Then the flesh wants to be touched by this attraction and will desire to have that thing that it'll give a sensuous or sensation feeling once again. Your soul got saved, *not* your flesh! We were made to feel. We must bring our flesh under subjection to the spirit man, daily.

Our nose is the organ we use to smell. Smell is also an aide in the ability to taste. When walking in the spirit, you can smell sin. Because your senses has been heightened in God. He will teach you how to see and smell spiritual things, His presence, as well as sin. The Bible says that God has nostrils and He uses them to smell for an aroma of Himself on you and me. You will be able to smell demons even if you don't understand what you smell. The Father will expose certain smells to you and tell you what not to eat, drink or even be around when there is a particular sin inhabiting a person, place or thing. Sin not only carries a weight, but it carries a smell that is transferable. It's a spiritual thing. Now, the point to the information given to you is this: because we are a three-part person (body, soul, and spirit), everything we do affects all of these parts.

In the 13th chapter of Judges, there is a story about a man named Samson. Samson, whose name in Hebrew means, *sun child, bright sun,*

Samson was ordained by God to be born for God's usage. He was marked by the Father. God told his parents to keep him from certain things. For now we will only discuss his hair and the woman, whose name is Delilah. Samson's hair was long and was to never be cut because his long hair carried God's anointing, thereby his strength and his hair was a consecration unto God; read and study this at your leisure.

Although Samson knew that he was a special child, he grew up with fleshy temptations and desires, much like all of us. After a time, Samson saw a woman who was not his wife that he was to have no parts of. She was not the blessing nor was she from his kinsmen. She worshipped other gods, but Samson's flesh desired her because of how she looked. Now as the story goes on, Delilah, whose name is Hebrew meaning *amorous, languishing and temptress*, was able to seduce Samson. He lay on her lap daily, and as he would lie there, she would stroke his hair, and he would tell her all his troubles. She captured him with her conversation (communication). This was the beginning of many mistakes, because his attention was no longer on his assignment, but his will to please another god, Delilah. As he spent more time with her, he became blinded by love or lust and desired to smell her, see her, and hear only her (he dismissed the correction from his leadership, his parents). Samson even desired her kisses (taste) more than anything else and those kisses of death caused him to spiral out of control.

These things were all spiritual. He did not know that he was being tricked by a seducing spirit and strong hold called Jezebel. There are many parts to this Jezebel spirit that we won't discuss here. This chapter is about you getting all of your strength up as Samson in the last chapter before it is too late. Now I know you are renewed in Christ. However, there is work you still must do. The problem with Samson is that he allowed himself to be drawn into a sexual relationship with Delilah and became soul-tied to her before she became his wife. It was all done by planted imagination. He, like us, was drawn away by his own lust and enticed, and then committed adultery against God. Samson probably thought to himself again; she looks *good* to me. How did he commit adultery against God? Samson was to stay sanctified and committed to God and only wed those of his own kinsman. Samson, you and I are set aside for God's usage. In order to be used and blessed by God, our spirits, souls, and bodies must be purified unto God.

Now, what you must do, my friend, if you have not already, divorce yourself from all the sexual partners you have ever had. Understand that the reason you must do this is because of the soul ties you carry. When you have been physically intimate with someone, their souls are still attached (if not delivered) to their last partners as well. In other words, if a woman has been with five men, those five men each have been with at least seven women each. Once you have been sexually intimate with them, you are attached to all of their partners' souls, too.

This stands to reason why oftentimes we will have a perverted dream about someone we have not been sexually involved with in 10 years and then we wonder why we had a dream about them that was sexual. Our souls are still with them! Any sexual soul tie can be a stronghold if it's an unlawful tie. Not only will these attachments keep you up at night, but they can make you have personality traits that are not necessarily a part of your genetic makeup. You can literally take on the habits, personality and thoughts of others. Your souls are intertwined with theirs.

I know this may seem a little farfetched, but it's spiritual and spirits, as you know, are real. We dwell in the spiritual world first; then the natural. This world is spiritual first, then natural. Everything we see in front of us in the natural is not the *real* world. There is one in the spirit realm, which is where God dwells; in the heavens. I hope this all make sense! That's because the real us lies in our soul. This is why He says that we must be born again, that we may go from corruptible to incorruptible. We will not make it to heaven with a corrupt spirit. Deliverance has to take place in order to be set free from sexual perversions.

There are sexual spirit demons that come to arouse you ladies and his name is Incubus. This demon will have sex with women while they sleep; I have experienced this early in my walk. Men, there is the Succubus sexual demon that comes to have sex with men while they sleep as well. Both of these types of demons take on the form a male or female predicated upon what your sexual preference is. There is also the marine water demon, which comes to show you all types of sexual perversion while you sleep and often shows up in your sleep or in the perversion of people. Here are a few scriptures for reference (Revelation 12:9, Genesis 3:1-4 Genesis 18 and 19 1-23 of the revised version).

Understand that all spirits can manifest themselves into or through humans. It was done all throughout the Bible, by God and the devil. I want you know that in order for the spirit to manifest, they need a body and they know that. It is unlawful for them to have access to us unless, there is a body present. So God and the devil use others to manifest through or to talk for them. Of course we know that God is the Creator of this (Jesus) and Satan is just an imitator of this (serpent in the garden). When in sexual sin, a lot of times we are hooked up to other people's images and not our own. We take on traits from someone else's spirits. Mothers, take notice when your baby girl all of a sudden start having sex and the sweet thing she was before starts to change. She becomes arrogant, bold, and disrespectful as if she has a decision-making voice in the house. This happens with boys as well. They have taken on someone's sexual trait. I know this might be a little deep for some. That's why it's imperative for us to go through deliverances to get free from our unsaved lifestyles.

There are so many perversions that can lie in the soul. Renouncing all sexual sins and getting your body parts back will not only free your soul, but this will free your mind as well. The devil is slick and he will continue to bring sexual thoughts about them to your mind. He is so sly that he will remind you and allow you to only think and dream about the sexual acts. Once you deny the devil entry, you can resist him into your spirit man, and he will flee…for a season. Therefore, you must renounce that marine spirit, that adultery spirit, that sexual stronghold and get rid of it. Beloved, if you are currently involved in a non-marital sexual relationship and can't seem to break away, it's because your soul is tied-up. Man or woman, you must get free!

I am not conveying to you something I read in a book, but I am conveying to you experience of getting free from soul-ties. I lived it and I got free. Not only am I free from sexual partners, but free from those who sexually abused me. I was having sexual nightmares of those past partners and those who attacked me. Now I am free. I implore you, by the grace of God, to stop where you are now in this and don't give the devil any more power to your sexual life; your body belongs to God. You must not allow "Delilah or David" to no longer have control of you. Get out of her lap, his lap, the lap of sexual deception! Yes, I am being very candid.

We need to be free from bonds and chains to serve God in spirit and in truth. Rescue yourself, my sister from the lap of Gregory, Daniel, Stephen and Jesse; my brother, rescue yourself from the lap of Shelly, Carol, Rose and Tammy. It is so detrimental to your growth in Christ. We are married to God and because He is a spirit and He lives in us. We commit spiritual adultery against Him and in Him, when we have sexual relations outside of marriage. It's as if we are having a threesome; Yuck! Yuck! You never thought about it that way, have you?

Example: God says He is married to the backslider. God says that He is coming back for

His bride. He is married to us and until we are *married* to someone else, then it becomes a threefold cord; and then the sexual bedroom acts are undefiled. At this point in your salvation, you are allowing others to defile you and the relationship with your Father, walk away and ask Him for forgiveness. Now go get your body parts back because they are spread all over this town and country. Call them back and release others so that you and they can be whole again. Yes, these dry bones can live again (Ezekiel 37:1-4). I have included a small prayer that you can say to help you get started.

Father, in the name of Jesus, I renounce sexual sin this day and I command my body parts to get away from every sexual partner who have known me. I command you to come out of my eye gate, my ear gate, and my nose. I command the taste of them to longer dwell in my mouth. I command that the touch of them to no longer be familiar within me. I command all my senses to dispose of sexual partners that were not properly acquired through marital ceremony. I plead the blood of Jesus against them and I close every door, in Jesus' name.

You can live saved, holy and free, After the Alter. Amen.

ACKNOWLEDGMENTS

First, to my wonderful and dynamic children; my first born, Jtoriauno G. (747), who made me a better woman when I laid eyes on that little face; you really do make me smile. Jaila M. (Bella), you are the princess I asked God for and even more. Jorddin S. (Mr. Spacely), you are absolutely my comedian; nobody makes me laugh like you do.

Secondly, to the Honorable Presiding Bishop of the Pentecostal Assemblies of the World, Bishop Charles H. Ellis. Thank you for instilling wisdom and fatherly love in me even when you didn't know it. You have taught me so much about excellence and servitude. Words cannot explain my appreciation and I have embraced all of your words with all my heart. To the woman who has taught me the real meaning of elegance and grace, regardless of life's circumstances, the First Lady of the Pentecostal Assembly of the World, First Lady Crisette M. Ellis.

Thirdly, to a woman who meant much to me, one I loved so dearly; my spiritual mother, Elizabeth "Mother Liz" Everson. She cheered me on constantly with this book and told me not to let her beat me in finishing a book. Needless to say, I lost that fight. I did not know we were racing against time. She finished hers before me and then left me, us. Mother Liz, you reminded me by saying, "If an old woman could do it, surely a young one can; now get to it!" I miss your smile and encouragement, but I know you're in His hands-the same hands that hold my heart every time I think of you.

Lastly, but certainly not least; to my best friend in the world who left me in 2005 to be with the Lord, Monique Deniko Bunch. I miss you a lot. Girl, you didn't get to see this project end; but you knew me.

~Prophetess Mary L. Hemmingway

ABOUT THE AUTHOR

Prophetess Mary L. Hemmingway is a true oracle of God, with over twenty-five years of ministry service. Prophetess Hemmingway was nurtured and taught in the Word of God by the late Bishop David L. Ellis of Greater Grace Temple, Detroit, MI. She continued in the ministry under the pastorate and tutelage of Bishop Charles H. Ellis III, Presiding Bishop of the Pentecostal Assemblies of the World, Inc. There she served in several ministry capacities which included the Greater Grace Temple Ministerial Staff.

A powerful herald of the gospel, she preaches with power and authority and takes no prisoners. She is gifted in spiritual warfare, evangelism, and teaching the Word of God to reach and win souls to Christ. People are her passion. She has an earned degree in Mental Health Counseling. Prophetess Mary L. Hemmingway is the founder and CEO of MLHG Ministries, LLC. Signs, miracles, and wonders in demonstration follow her along with her cadency, boldness, and transparency to reach souls which makes her sought after globally. Pastor Mary L. Hemmingway is the pastor of Refiners Fire Ministries, has three adult children, and resides in Detroit, Michigan.

CONNECT WITH THE AUTHOR

If you would like to reach the author, kindly send an email to godbranded@gmail.com with your specific request and/or comments.

www.ingramcontent.com/pod-product-compliance
Lightning Source LLC
LaVergne TN
LVHW051549070426
835507LV00021B/2485